THE DEATH AND LIFE
OF AMERICAN LABOR

THE DEATH AND LIFE OF AMERICAN LABOR

Toward a New Workers' Movement

Stanley Aronowitz

VERSO

London • New York

First published by Verso 2014

1 3 5 7 9 10 8 6 4 2

Verso
UK: 6 Meard Street, London W1F 0EG
US: 20 Jay Street, Suite 1010, Brooklyn, NY 11201
www.versobooks.com

Verso is the imprint of New Left Books

ISBN-13: 978-1-78168-138-1 (HB)
eISBN-13: 978-1-78168-194-7 (US)
eISBN-13: 978-1-78478-007-4 (UK)

British Library Cataloguing in Publication Data

Aronowitz, Stanley.
The death and life of American labor : toward a new worker's movement / Stanley
Aronowitz.
pages cm
Includes index.
Summary: "Union membership in the United States has fallen below 11 percent, the
lowest rate since before the New Deal. Longtime scholar of the American union movement
Stanley Aronowitz argues that the labor movement as we have known it for most of the
last 100 years is effectively dead. And he asserts that this death has been a long time
coming—the organizing principles chosen by the labor movement at midcentury have
come back to haunt the movement today. In an expansive survey of new initiatives, strikes,
organizations and allies Aronowitz analyzes the possibilities of labor's renewal, and sets
out a program for a new, broad, radical workers' movement"—Provided by publisher.
ISBN 978-1-78168-138-1 (hardback)—ISBN 978-1-78168-194-7 (ebk)
1. Labor movement—United States—History—21st century. 2. Labor—United States—
History—21st century. 3. Labor unions—United States—History—21st century. I. Title.
HD8072.5.A759 2014
331.880973—dc23
2014018867

Library of Congress Cataloging-in-Publication Data
A catalog record for this book is available from the Library of Congress.

Typeset in Minion Pro by Hewer Text UK Ltd, Edinburgh, Scotland
Printed in the US by Maple Press

Contents

Union Defeat at Volkswagen

A merica is a winner-take-all culture. Some European countries allow proportional representation, recognizing the right of minority unions to participate in legislatures and collective bargaining, but not the United States. The landmark National Labor Relations Act of 1935 mandated our current playbook for union representation, in effect reversing a century of plural unionism in many workplaces. Under the law, although more than one union can vie for the right to represent a single bargaining unit, if the petitioner seeks exclusive representation then ultimately the unit can only be represented by a single union. Thus the minority organization is excluded from participation in collective bargaining and other shop-floor matters until the contract termination, after which it can seek, via an election supervised by the Labor Board, to replace the prevailing monopoly labor organization with a monopoly of its own. Before the postwar era, many unions sought minority bargaining rights, but abandoned this strategy in favor of winner take all.[1]

Long neglected by organized labor, the largely nonunion South has finally become a focus of interest for the United Auto Workers. More than a decade ago, the UAW was soundly defeated in two board election bids to organize the Nissan plant in Smyrna, Tennessee, and until recently it refrained from risking a third humiliation. However, by the 2000s, thirteen European and Japanese car companies had opened assembly plants in the American South and border states. Nissan,

Mercedes, Toyota, and Volkswagen are among the foreign companies that have transplanted some of their facilities to the United States. And the South has been a favored corporate target for obvious reasons: all Southern states and some border states have "right to work" laws that prohibit the union shop, and the region's antiunion environment in general is stifling; the states' governments are eager to provide huge cash grants to corporations that locate there; and taxes are generally much lower than in the Northeast and Midwest or on the West Coast. General Motors and Ford, too, have closed numerous plants in the Northeast and Midwest and built new facilities in the South for these reasons and more.

The South has some of the characteristics of an internal colony. It is a historically agricultural region whose residents earn significantly lower incomes than their Northern counterparts. Its geography includes sparsely populated areas that have long suffered sporadic, seasonal, and low-wage employment, making them highly favorable for plant location. The UAW sanctioned these moves by U.S. companies as long as the companies agreed to allow unionization. But the transplanted factories have mostly resisted becoming union shops even when their home-base factories are unionized. The expanding number of transplants forced a reluctant UAW to reconsider its organizing program and to venture south.

For several years UAW has conducted four Southern organizing campaigns—at Nissan's huge plant in Canton, Mississippi; at Mercedes's Alabama factory; Nissan again at Smyrna; and at the Volkswagen assembly plant near Chattanooga, Tennessee, which employs 1,550 workers. The union has declared that it will not seek bargaining rights under the law until a company enters a "neutrality" agreement. Nissan has displayed characteristic hostility to unionization, refusing to grant even a neutrality agreement, one in which the company pledges not to interfere with the union's organizing effort. Volkswagen, however, was glad to agree to noninterference. Its German facilities are all represented by the powerful metalworkers union, IG Metall, which has made its position on the fate of transplants clear: Do not interfere with union organizing unless you, the company, wish to court trouble. And the company, all of whose other plants have works councils, is intensely interested in installing one in the

Chattanooga factory. But under U.S. labor law, a works council, which represents both management and labor, cannot be started unless the plant's workers have union representation.

Consequently, when the union's campaign was in high gear, not only did the company refrain from the usual antiunion ploys—threats of plant removal, intimidation of activists, and attacks against the union as an illegitimate "outsider"—it even awarded union representatives access to the plant to talk to the workers and hold organizing meetings. Prior to the election, more than two-thirds of the workers signed union cards. Based on conventional wisdom, everyone, including the organizers, confidently predicted a UAW victory. This confidence was not severely shaken by an outburst of vehement opposition from the state's governor, one of its U.S. senators, and a relatively small inside group of antiunion rank-and-file workers. But a week before the scheduled vote, union organizers sensed a turn of the tide. Their anxiety proved to be justified. On February 14, 2014,[2] the union lost the election by 86 votes out of more than 1,300 cast. Yet the real margin was only 44 votes, for if these had gone to the union column, the UAW would have prevailed.

The major networks, the *New York Times* and other leading metropolitan newspapers, and labor experts—historians and pundits—took the result as a crushing defeat for the union and gravely commented that what happened would make labor's future Southern organizing a steep uphill journey. UAW president Bob King agreed with this ominous diagnosis. Indeed, after getting into bed with the company and enjoying in-plant access, union leaders might well have been disappointed in the result. But there is another possible interpretation of it. The UAW had not sought a secret ballot in an election for any transplanted workplace for more than a decade and labor has generally avoided Southern organizing for much longer than that, so the union might have heralded the close vote as an inspiring beginning. It might have declared its intention to stay in the community and form a local union, charged modest dues to those workers who joined, and, eventually, demanded minority representation. But in the immediate aftermath of the election, union response reflected the gloom-and-doom commentary of conservative and liberal media. The winner-take-all mentality, pervasive in labor's ranks, overcame the radical imagination.

There is, of course, a major problem when a single union organizes in the South or a rural area. Through the CIO's insurgency in the 1930s; during Operation Dixie shortly after World War II, in the 1980s in South Carolina, where the AFL-CIO focused on the Greenville-Spartanburg area's sprawling textile industry, individual unions banded together to mount a coordinated campaign, rather than going it alone. Today, in the 2010s, there is little or no talk about creating a new labor environment through coordination. Each shop is on its own, and organizing has a discrete, single-valence orientation. Though Operation Dixie was largely unsuccessful and the South Carolina campaign was an outright flop, the principle involved in each effort was valid. Labor itself has to declare that it is entering the South in a big way, that it is prepared to put millions of dollars and hundreds of organizers into the field, and that it will focus on building a major social presence in the region that addresses all aspects of workers' lives, not only the shop floor. We are a long way from implementing this vision, or even debating it. Despite brave words from AFL-CIO headquarters, unions rely on the mainstream political power structure rather than on their own resources for gains. They have poured hundreds of millions into electing Democrats to national and state offices and relegated the grassroots organization of workers to the margins. Make no mistake. The major unions have the money to organize, but their strategy has shifted decisively to the political arena.

In this regard it is worthwhile to recollect that minority unions, many of them without collective bargaining agreements, were common before the Labor Relations Act became law. Since then, eager to achieve stability and peace, nearly all unions in manufacturing, private retail services, entertainment, technical services, and the public sector have chosen the winner-take-all path, signed increasingly long-term collective bargaining agreements banning strikes for the duration of the contract, and yielded to management demands for wage and work-rule concessions, not only during recessions but also in flush times. The typical contract also concedes management's right to direct the workforce as it pleases; the union may grieve unfair practices, but under such agreements they are in no position to contest management's prerogatives.

These concessions were part of the legacy that UAW brought to Chattanooga. Since the financial crisis of 2008 the autoworkers' union has conceded to the big three U.S. auto companies' demand for a two-tier wage system: new employees in the bargaining unit can expect to earn $15 to $17 an hour instead of the $28-an-hour prevailing rate. The UAW has also relaxed enforcement of work rules and agreed to higher worker contributions to the pension plan and health benefits. In the few instances where it has been forced to strike to protect its gains, such as at the earth moving–equipment giant Caterpillar, it has been badly beaten, called off the strikes, and signed long-term contracts under extremely unfavorable conditions. In short, the union has drawn close to the companies it does business with, in the hope that union concessions will result in union preservation.

Although VW remained silent about these features of current UAW policy, the antiunion forces did not ignore them. The media has concentrated on the effect of the antagonism of outside politicians, but there has been little analysis of the relative importance of the in-plant antiunion forces to the outcome. Even so, 632 workers voted to be represented by UAW, almost half of the more than 1,300 voters. Indeed, some workers may have been following the company's lead to vote for union representation, but the closeness of the outcome was a testament to the resolve of many workers to have a union in spite of the union's detractors. These yes votes are a base upon which the UAW can build, unless it follows the infamous widespread union practice of leaving town after an NLRB (National Labour Relations Board) defeat. Of course, maintaining an active campaign in the absence of a union contract and regular dues payments is an expensive proposition, even for relatively wealthy unions. Yet the South, always the Achilles heel of the labor movement, is now the weakest point in a generally weakened frame. If organized labor fails to root itself in key Southern cities and rural areas, it will die.

Which raises another question: Is holding a Labor Board–supervised election the best strategy for union organization? Over more than thirty years it has become apparent to unionists, experienced observers, and historians that even under Democratic national administrations the election route is deeply problematic, because employers today have many tactics at their disposal to delay a vote and to influence or intimidate workers—tactics that include the threat to remove a plant if the union comes in. In the case of VW, the company's neutrality may have vitiated the effect of such tactics, but that did not prevent others from engaging in them. Although threats and delays are routine features of labor board elections and experienced organizations generally know how to counter them, in this Southern city antiunion tactics were employed within and without the plant that could not fail to do serious harm. The union's decision to seek an election had been influenced by circumstances so apparently favorable that organizers refrained from using radio and other media to promote their cause and even agreed not to conduct visits to workers' homes, evidently believing that their work inside the plant was sufficient. There were other paths not taken: asking the company to agree to a card check; seeking a minority union agreement; refraining from asking for legal representation until a solid union culture had been in play for a period of time; building a local union without official standing.

That these strategies were not considered, at least not openly, testifies to the limits of the organizers' imagination. There is also conclusive evidence that at the deepest level the UAW and most other unions are no longer viewed by workers, including their own members, as a militant force. To be sure, the union might benefit from a neutrality agreement by the company, but such agreements are liable to be viewed as a symptom of company unionism, because they make it impossible for a campaign to use forceful rhetoric and can engender hostility among workers who have reason not to trust the company.

This book is a sustained argument that the era of labor-management cooperation that was initiated by the New Deal and supported by succeeding legislation and that saw general cooperation from the unions has come to an end. Consequently, to rely on the institutional framework established by the Labor Relations Act has thwarted and will continue to thwart the ability of workers and their unions to meet the challenges created by globalization and its significantly aggravated antiunion and antiworker political and social environment. In the following pages, I explore the ideological and political contexts facing the workers' movements and make some proposals for addressing the challenges they imply. My deepest aspiration is to help generate a discussion of what exists and what is to be done, now.

I have some debts to acknowledge in preparing this book: Steve Brier made extensive comments and suggestions for the first six chapters. Michael Pelias read the entire manuscript and like Steve made significant improvements. Laura McClure read the first four chapters and helped deepen the argument. And Penny Lewis read portions of the manuscript and, beyond this contribution, was largely responsible for provoking me to write it.

An Institution
Without a Vision

The development of the U.S. labor movement might be divided into three phases. During the first, the period between the late colonial era (the early 1770s) and the founding of the American Federation of Labor (AFL) in 1886, "organized labor" was not only concerned with wages and working conditions but also had broader interests. In the 1830s and 1840s, based on the premise that workers needed to be literate, labor organizations fought for free public education for the first six grades. Early unions formed their own local political parties but at the national level supported the Democrats, one of whom, Andrew Jackson, enacted universal male suffrage. From time to time workers also attempted to organize a national labor union, but these efforts were largely unsuccessful. The one exception—the Knights of Labor—survived for a generation, from the 1870s through the 1890s. The Knights were democratic insofar as their local assemblies were open to all workers, blacks as well as whites, regardless of craft or industry. Only lawyers and clergy were excluded.

The founding of the AFL marked the beginning of the second phase. The United Mineworkers was virtually the only industrial union in the AFL. When AFL president Samuel Gompers sponsored industrial organizing in the meatpacking industry in 1917 and the steel industry two years later, these were exceptions to the common practice that organized labor consisted in craftsmen who required little or no govern-ment assistance to form their organizations.

The third phase began in the New Deal era. Legislation, particularly the National Labor Relations Act (1935) introduced secret ballot elec-tion, supervised by the federal government, as a secure mechanism for letting workers choose an "appropriate unit" for union representation: whether they wanted union representation and, in the event of compe-tition, which union they preferred. But the NLRA, went further: it promoted collective bargaining as the legitimate institution for the resolution of labor disputes.[1]

The passage of the NLRA did not occur in a vacuum. The bill was introduced after two years of intense labor struggles: the miners' and apparel workers' strikes of 1933; the two brilliantly successful 1934 general strikes, in San Francisco and Minneapolis, and the nearly general strike in Toledo, Ohio, all of which were led by the left; and the national textile strike, called by the AFL affiliate, that brought 400,000 workers out of the factories, especially women from the South. This strike failed when President Roosevelt asked the union to call it off, promising to bring the textile corporations to the bargaining table. The AFL United Textile Workers agreed, but Roosevelt did not keep his side of the deal. The companies launched a vendetta against union militants; more than 7,000 were blacklisted and forced to leave the company towns, a migration that permanently sullied subsequent organizing campaigns in the South. Nevertheless, the union wagon rolled on. The great sit-down strikes, or factory occupations, in rubber (in 1936) and the auto industries that predated the Supreme Court's legalization of the NLRA in 1937 were resolved by recognition agreements. The typical contract in 1936 and 1937 simply recognized the union for the purposes of negotiating wages and working conditions, without further specifica-tion. But the NLRA was proclaimed by AFL president William Green as labor's Magna Carta, and the newly formed industrial unions gathered into the Committee for Industrial Organization[2] were committed to collective bargaining and employed the strike only as a last resort.

When a reporter asked Samuel Gompers, the founding and long-time AFL president about the long-term goals of American labor, his famous one-word answer was "More." He firmly rejected any long-term vision for the labor movement. From the 1890s through World War I the Socialists led a quarter of AFL affiliates, representing more than 300,000 members, including the Machinists, Garment Workers, Brewery Workers, Western Federation of Miners (metal), Tailors, and Bakery Workers had significant influence in others, like the Painters and United Mineworkers (coal) and in a dozen important labor councils.[3]

Even though the left was never strong enough to capture AFL leadership and was divided on the Socialist Party's relationship to the labor movement, it remained an important source of financial, industrial, and political support for strikes. Indeed, its perennial presidential candidate Eugene V. Debs was a former militant union leader and gave many speeches in behalf of workers and their unions. The Socialist Party's split on labor involved five key questions: (1) whether the labor movement should renounce craft unionism in favor of industrial unions that united workers in a single workplace and industry, regardless of occupation; (2) whether to challenge the conservative Gompers and his craft-union base in the AFL; (3) whether to form a new industrial union (in fact, Debs attended the first meeting of the radicals who founded the IWW); (4) how far to press the Socialist program of political action, as the AFL had refused early on to engage in party politics even to organize a labor party; and (5) whether to openly advocate revolutionary socialism within the labor movement. Note that *revolutionary* did not necessarily connote violence but simply the aim of creating a "cooperative commonwealth" in which all productive property would be held by the common rather than by private interests. While not renouncing reforms within the prevailing capitalist system, Socialists saw the labor movement as a component of that commonwealth, at least in terms of workers' self-management of the decisive means of production.

With the notable exception of the industrial-versus-craft union argument, these ideological debates effectively ended in the aftermath of World War I. Gompers had already reversed himself about political neutrality in 1908, when the AFL backed William Jennings Bryan's unsuccessful Democratic presidential run, and the labor movement remained safely in that party's camp for most of the twentieth century.[4] Gompers also sponsored the organization of unskilled and semiskilled industrial workers in the packinghouse and steel industries. Perhaps equally important, mainstream labor had openly embraced capitalism, while becoming both a fervent advocate and client of social reform.

In 1919, the newly formed Communist Party declared for the transformation of the unions, but aside from its revolutionary rhetoric, in practical terms the party became a key advocate of industrial unionism. Even so, Communists were expelled from most AFL unions for their adherence to the Communist International, and spent much of the 1920s and early 1930s engaged in assisting workers who fought defensive battles. Under the banner of the Trade Union Education League (TUEL), they supported and organized textile and apparel workers in the South who resisted wage cuts, most famously in Gastonia, North Carolina; exiled from the trade unions, despite their strategy of "boring from within" the established unions, eventually they also formed independent unions in several industries, notably for metalworkers, autoworkers, textile and garment workers, dockworkers and woodworkers in the Northwest. But neither the socialists nor the communists within the unions went beyond education and agitation in challenging labor's fundamental commitment to the existing system. For the leading Communist trade union figure, William Z. Foster, industrial unionism was a premier radical act; he had been a revolutionary syndicalist before joining the party, and his history afterward remained syndicalist, despite his presidential candidacy in 1932.[5]

The crucial turning point for nearly all radicals, however, occurred with two historic developments: the New Deal, particularly the enactment of the National Labor Relations Act in 1935; and, in the same year, the announcement by the CP leadership reversing its ritual denunciation of the Socialists as social fascists and expressing its desire to form a united front of all working-class and progressive forces to fight fascism.

The NLRA recognized workers' right to form unions of their own choosing, to take "concerted action" to win union demands, and to negotiate with employers over wages, working conditions and other issues of mutual interest. The NLRA did not mandate that union labor and employers reach a collective bargaining agreement, but it did make negotiations with a union that had won a representation election compulsory—a matter of law, not voluntarism—if the union showed majority support in a unit deemed by the Labor Relations Board appropriate for collective bargaining. The Labor Relations Board was established by government not only to determine this eligibility but also to administer the representation election; it also adjudicated "unfair labor practices" that might thwart labor's right to form independent unions. It is worth noting that the ACLU opposed the NLRA, on the grounds that the law granted exclusive bargaining rights only to victorious unions. But most unions wanted exclusive representation because they feared that a plurality of representatives would open the door to the company unions that had been dominant in the 1920s. Exclusive bargaining proved a boon for the formation of a strong labor bureaucracy, but it limited workers' ability to choose alternatives when the union failed to support their struggles. Even so, the NLRA provided for the possibility of minority unionism, an option few labor organizations took. We shall revisit the question of minority unionism in the last chapter.

From 1938, when after a series of court challenges the NLRA was finally made legal by the Supreme Court, to the present day, collective bargaining within the framework of the labor relations law has been the accepted union practice. As we shall see, recognizing the limitations of acting strictly within the law, some workers' organizations—including a few established unions—have preferred to strike for recognition rather than follow the rule of winning an NLRB-supervised election for exclusive bargaining rights. And they have not always done so assuming that they would then negotiate and administer a contract with the employer(s). But the rule still obtains, even for rank-and-file movements, whose demands are generally framed in terms of getting a decent contract, and for decades there has been almost no challenge to the principle of exclusive bargaining. Neither has there been much challenge within the movement to traditional politics. Although some oppositional groups do not agree in principle with the established leadership's adherence to the Democratic Party, wherever they have achieved local or national union office they have operated within the law.

Criticisms aside, organized labor is integrated into the prevailing political and economic system; so much so that it not only complies with the law but also lacks an ideology opposed to the prevailing capitalist system. Integration has even led to cooperative relationships between union leaderships and the companies with which they deal. Company-union collaborations are symptoms of nearly all unions' loss of class perspective. Corporate capital, on the other hand, knows it is a class and acts accordingly. Unions have renounced class warfare, while their adversaries pursue it with a vengeance—against the workers unions are supposed to represent and defend.

Recently, some public-employee unions and the Occupy Wall Street movement have challenged the cautious, even passive stance of most of the unions on the increasing centralization of wealth. In late November 2011, activists of West Coast Occupy Wall Street called upon unions and nonunion workers to engage in a general strike on December 12 in Oakland to protest the growing gap between the very rich and the rest of us. But the leadership of the International Longshore and Warehouse Union (ILWU), Occupy's most reliable labor ally, declared it would not participate. For a historical context, it is important to recall that when, during the 1999 mass protests against the World Trade Organization, unions like the United Steelworkers marched alongside the militants who literally shut down Seattle's downtown, the ILWU went a step further, using its power to shut down all West Coast ports for a day, a stroke of exemplary solidarity. The Longshore union's decision in 2011 *not* to support the call for a general strike was influenced by two factors. First, as is the case with nearly all unions that sign collective bargaining agreements, the ILWU is bound by a clause barring strikes during the life of its current contract; the last time ILWU had supported a shutdown of the Oakland port, it was fined $65,000. Second, a "general strike" requires a measure of labor unity on a series of demands and grievances and the protection that comes from mass worker participation. These conditions were present in the great 1934 San Francisco general strike, which was initiated and led by dockworkers but quickly joined by almost all of the area's labor organizations. Although the Occupy movement's attack on the gross inequalities perpetrated by finance capital and its political allies in both parties drew widespread support, including a degree of labor solidarity, a bold action such as a general strike entails raising the struggle to a new level.

That is not yet in the cards. For more than seventy-five years, the labor movement by law and by custom has been enclosed by and restricted to collective bargaining, with the goal of achieving a contract that seals in wages, benefits, a grievance procedure and specified work rules. In return for that security, workers and their union agree, crucially, to surrender their First Amendment right to withhold their labor.[6] The penalties for violating these unconstitutional agreements are often severe: stiff fines, imprisonment of union officials and sometimes, as after the three-day walkout by New York City transit workers, a court order barring the automatic check-off of union dues.[7]

When in 2011 Wisconsin governor Scott Walker and his allies in the state legislature outlawed collective bargaining, public workers, unionists and their allies flooded Madison, staging huge protests, most notably an occupation of the state capitol. It was a remarkable demonstration, but still largely a defensive one. Except for a brief moment when the labor council president for the Madison area suggested the possibility of a general strike, there was little debate about the limits of contract unionism, the core of which is the no-strike clause.

At this juncture, we need to ask, What are the limits of the contract? And to deal with the question of those limits—what the contract is not and cannot do—we must first define what it is and does.

The contract is a compromise between labor and an employer, private or public. The workers agree to suspend most of their demands for a designated period of time, which grows longer in duration every contract season. In the past decade, that period has grown to as much as six years. Even if working conditions change, the employees cannot reopen the contract unless the employer consents. The contract has the force of law, and its violation can lead to serious consequences.

The union is responsible for enforcing the contract, and for disciplining workers who violate the agreement through direct action. Of course, companies and state administrations themselves regularly bypass or brazenly violate the contract. To remedy these infractions, the union can grieve and finally arbitrate the violations. Increasingly, the arbitration process has been heavily weighted on the employers' side, but workers have no other recourse, under the law of the contract.

Consequently, if their issues are sufficiently serious, workers sometimes engage in wildcat walkouts and other job actions, such as work-to-rule or sabotage.[8] Their union is obliged to renounce the strike or job action, and must "order" workers back to the job. Ironically, under the law the union acts as management's police force.

Under these conditions, the union tends to become conservative and can even become an agent of shop floor worker subordination. A minority of shop floor leaders and some officials do resist, but the weight of the law mostly prevails. Thanks to the weakening of workers' rights—during economic booms as well as busts—collective bargaining is now mostly a kind of collective begging. Yet for most union officials and activists, collective bargaining remains a sacred cow to be cherished in the name of worker security. And, of course, as conservative state legislatures try to emulate Wisconsin's and Indiana's abolition of public employees' collective bargaining rights, we can expect the next period of labor action to be a fierce struggle to preserve existing bargaining rights, even though employers in the private and public sectors have long exhibited their contempt for the institution and have ceaselessly undermined its dialogic assumption.

Few unionists are willing to advocate for the abolition of restrictions on strikes, let alone aggressively fight for it. Until the 1930s the labor agreement was fairly rare, but the labor movement has forgotten its own traditions. Once workers—and not only IWW members—struck for their demands and agreed to return to work only when the demands were met[9] or the strike was lost. I do not expect contracts to be retired anytime soon— employers need them as much as union officials—but labor could fight for the reinstatement of the unrestricted strike. Critics of this position ask why employers would sign contracts at all if by doing so they could not buy labor peace. The answer is fairly straight-forward: power. What really determines labor relations is the strength of the workers and their unions. In Europe, unions do not typically agree to strike limitations. In the United States, labor's back is and long has been against the wall, and now some unions have reached out to new allies: students, the Occupy movement, workers' centers, community organizations and progressive intellectuals. However, until and unless unions reexamine the historical shifts that have led to their own unprecedented weakness—including the traps of collective bargaining, exclusive bargaining rights, and no-strike agreements—their multidecade slide will accelerate, and we will see disembodied impotent demonstrations become commonplace and substantial gains for workers in real terms more and more rare.

The conventional wisdom among labor activists and labor intellectuals is that even though, as C. Wright Mills said more than sixty years ago, "the union bureaucracy stands between the company bureaucracy [or the government bureaucracy] and the rank and file of the workers, operating as a shock absorber of both," and often takes a stance of collaboration with owners and top managers, though it is also an instrument of the workers' struggle.[10] Accordingly, the contract protects workers' wages, benefits and working conditions. And defenders of the system note that although the grievance procedure is flawed, largely because management can delay addressing claims and because the union must share the high costs of arbitration, individual and departmental injustices can be resolved in workers' favor. Moreover, some argue, if the union has an effective steward system, many issues on the shop or office floor may be solved without recourse to cumbersome formal procedures. But that is a big if. There are some unions that encourage strong shop or office floor leaders, but most now rely on fulltime business agents or representatives to address ordinary grievances, and many unions employ lawyers to do it, a policy that reproduces what I call the awe of the law. This disempowers the rank and file and strengthens the authority of the labor bureaucracy.

Defenders of organized labor's decision to ally itself with the Democratic Party rely on two arguments: (1) labor's involvement in the political system tends to reduce the effectiveness of the most determined antiunion forces at the national and state levels; (2) since labor relations is always a three-way proposition—the third actor is the state—unions cannot avoid intervening in politics.

The long arm of the state and its repressive apparatuses is one of the compelling reasons for labor's political role. Another is the imperative to preserve—never mind advance—social welfare gains such as Social Security, Medicare and Medicaid, and unemployment compensation, all of which are ceaselessly threatened by the right. All defenders of labor's alliance with the Democrats remind detractors that the DP is the only game in town and labor is not strong enough to create its own political party. Hence, the AFL-CIO and its ostensible rival, Change to Win, are formally part of the DP, a relationship that all but prohibits the unions from publicly disagreeing with the party. And since the DP has generally become center-right—willing to compromise major elements of the social welfare state such as Social Security and Medicare and pursue an aggressive war-oriented foreign program—whatever resolutions the unions may pass at their conventions, in practice they have become politically centrist as well.

Arguments for Democratic affiliation ignore another option: to revert to a time when, at least in principle, the labor movement was not formally integrated into any political party, even if it occasionally made endorsements. In New York State, where almost a quarter of the waged population are union members, the progressive unions once helped form the Socialist Party, which was a real force in New York City politics until the early 1920s. In the 1930s they organized the American Labor Party as a goad to the graft-ridden Democrats, although at the state level they rarely expressed their disaffection by running their own candidates. In New York City, the ALP did put up candidates for city council, became a partner in the fusion candidacy of Mayor LaGuardia, and competed vigorously with the Democrats. Unfortunately, today's Working Families Party is a reliable Democratic shill, except upstate, where it can sometimes run its own candidates without jeopardizing a Democrat's chances of election.

Union subordination to the all but incapacitated Labor Relations Act has combined with this deference to the Democrats to alter our evaluation of a union's twofold character. Unions today are primarily what Louis Althusser once termed "ideological state apparatuses." But beyond their ideological role they have been integrated into the capitalist system and the capitalist state in particular. Of course, this integration does not preclude their maintaining some degree of conflict with the systems within which they operate. However, as we shall see, because union contracts are more long-term, the national and international unions no longer pose a serious threat to the corporations with whom they deal, and at least since the disastrous discharge of striking Air Traffic controllers in 1981, they have faithfully refrained from challenging the no-strike provisions of federal and state laws.

Although the incredible shrinkage of the strike weapon may be ascribed to economic stagnation and domestic decline, the national union bureaucracies have also played a role by thwarting local initiatives and undermining the use of direct action—strikes and job actions—as an instrument of workers' struggles. Their virtual abandonment of organizing, and especially their failure to organize the growing precariat of contingent, temporary and part-time workers; Southern labor; and the professionals (except for teachers) who effectively control the labor process in numerous industries make their own shrinkage inevitable.[11]

This failure to organize and to fight does not reflect a lack of resources, but instead a lack of faith. Most unions have agreed to and implemented the prevailing strategy: relying on electoral politics to achieve their objective, which is merely defensive. They are trying to keep the wolf from the door. That their presumed benefactors, the centrist political elite, evince little desire to identify themselves with workers' interests does not seem to deter the unions from heaping huge sums of money on mainstream national and state candidates. In short, the labor leaders have so closed the distance between themselves and the various institutions of national and international power that *labor movement* used to describe the organizations they represent, is now an oxymoron.

Neither the United Auto Workers (UAW) nor the United Steelworkers (USW) ever systematically addressed the severe managerial shortcomings that hobbled their employers and by the late 1980s resulted in mass layoffs. Instead, as we shall see in Chapter 5, they *adapted* to industry changes via job security agreements rather than attempting to *intervene in the development of the changes themselves*. They were prisoners of the doctrine of "management prerogatives," according to which workers and their unions are prohibited by mutual agreement from challenging investment decisions, price policy and profits. Private property and the law had become sacred, subject neither to collective bargaining nor to labor's broader program. This doctrine put organized labor in a narrow position on the shop floor and in politics as well. Unions accepted the limitations imposed on them without much protest.[12] They became what C. Wright Mills termed "dependent variables" in the political economy.[13] The precipitous decline of the unions needs explanation beyond contingency or a casting of good guys and villains. Their refusal to transform themselves into a labor movement or, more accurately, to return to the principles and aims of the labor movement's great era cannot be attributed only to the perfidy of oligarchical leaders. Nor is it enough to cite the globalization of the economy. These factors have certainly contributed to labor's decline, but they are not the whole story.

And this book is not simply an analysis of that decline, but also an examination of the problems and promise of a new labor movement. In later chapters I discuss current efforts to reverse more than thirty years of retreat and I propose steps toward that goal that are not yet on the agendas of even the most farsighted and militant factions, who though they are demanding to put the "movement back into the unions" are not prepared to transgress the rules of the current debate. Perhaps this book can stimulate struggles that through practice will become realistic once more. By demanding the impossible, we make it possible.

CHAPTER ONE

The Winter of Our Discontent

The year 2011 seemed to launch a new era of popular unrest. Europe was roiled by protests against the relentless march of neoliberal austerity policies, policies directed principally at the living standards of the working classes and salaried middle classes both. European unions and left-wing political parties took to the streets in vigorous protest against conservative efforts to cut wages and roll back social welfare. On the other side of the Atlantic, where the people are hopelessly fragmented, most Americans suffered quietly or internalized their anger by blaming themselves for unemployment, foreclosed homes, and wage erosion. Many today still harbor hope that their slide from comfort to poverty will be halted and then reversed by their economic masters and center-right political leaders, despite overwhelming evidence that corporate capitalist and state efforts to address the crisis are directed upward toward large-scale financial institutions and manufacturing giants. Indeed, watching U.S. workers as they experienced four decades of retrenchment of pay, social services, education and other aspects of the social wage has convinced many observers that the American people are either infinitely patient or else predisposed to fix blame on immigrants, blacks, Latinos, terrorists, and other "others," or on themselves, or anywhere except where it belongs.

However, in 2011, in a rare moment, suddenly public issues were not rehearsed as private troubles. Passivity and displacement took a backseat to the first major outburst of opposition in more than three decades. It was a cry of resistance heard round the world and it undermined the official claim that the United States is the exception to the rule that most societies are rent and class-divided. At least for now, there is general recognition that we are no exception. Even so, national beliefs die hard. Our students still march to institutions of postsecondary schooling and graduate professional training as if there were good jobs at the end of the long slog. Our ideologies often precede and survive the conditions that produce and legitimate them.

Our current awakening began in one of the more turbulent regions of the country, the contentious state of Wisconsin, home of legendary political figures of all stamps: the progressive Senator Robert La Follette, the Socialists who governed Milwaukee for decades, until the 1950s, and the nefarious Senator Joseph McCarthy and his far-right successors. In February 2011 the state's public employees and their unions—backed by other unions, political progressives, and students, many of whom were themselves unionized public employees, members of the Teaching Assistants Association at the University of Wisconsin—met Wisconsin's Republican governor Scott Walker and his state senate allies' bold abolition of public-sector collective bargaining with mass demonstrations that lasted for weeks and staged an occupation of the state senate chambers. At the height of the action, perhaps 100,000 workers and their allies had filled Madison's streets and the capitol's halls. And this protest was not the usual one-shot affair; it grew in early spring to a statewide movement, one that witnessed teacher-motivated school walkouts in many of the state's cities and towns, backed by the unionized graduate students at the university. Midway during the demonstrations, the Madison-area AFL-CIO president openly suggested a general strike. When fourteen Democratic senators disappeared, denying the governor the needed quorum to vote on his collective-bargaining ban, it appeared that the general strike was imminent. The Madison-area labor council appointed a committee to implement the strike. Then adroit Democratic leaders stepped in to propose a recall movement, directed at four GOP senators who had won office by slim margins, and at the governor himself. This move diverted the forward march of the protest to electoral channels, and the general strike was suspended, although some direct action continued. The recall effort deposed two senators, not enough to reverse the right wing's majority. In Ohio, voters that November repealed a similar state law by a solid two-thirds majority. But in Wisconsin, a second recall effort against Governor Walker in 2012 failed, and the forward march of the movement was halted.

Reflections on the Madison Uprising

One of the chief characteristics of United States labor and social history is that workers and other oppressed and discriminated formations will absorb prolonged assaults on their working and living conditions before they protest and resist. Mass industrial unionism rose in this country after seventy years of relentless worker exploitation— miserable working conditions, frequent wage cuts, brutal killings and firings of union militants by steel, meatpacking, automobile, and rubber barons. The 1930s labor upsurge occurred only after five years of the deepest depression in the history of capitalism. But when it began to gain traction, the rebellion spread with lightning speed. Within a decade after the first mass strikes in the coal mining and apparel industries, in 1933, union membership, as Peter Rachleff shows, had multiplied from 2 million to more than 14 million.[1]

In the 1970s and 1980s, labor's forward march slowed and then halted. The ostensible cause was the fiscal crisis in state and local communities, which politicians, the mainstream media, and many economists ascribed to the disparity between rising public-sector labor costs and restricted tax revenues. Since this was also the period when many manufacturing facilities began migrating from the Northeast and Midwest to the American and global South, many cities and towns, in the vain hope of reversing or slowing down capital flight, scrambled to offer tax advantages, subsidies, and infrastructural concessions to business interests. Meanwhile, school budgets were slashed, some hospitals were closed, and local street and highways remained unrepaired.

A new pattern of concessionary bargaining arose, with New York public unions in the vanguard. In 1976, when Wall Street refused to extend loans to the city government to meet payroll and other expenses—a virtual capital strike—the 150,000-member District Council 37 and other public sector unions agreed to let the city government lay off 50,000 mostly "provisional" (non–civil service) workers, that is, more than 20 percent of the municipal labor force, and hand over control of the city's finances to the financial services sector. Throughout the 1980s, such concessionary bargaining remained the rule. The decade of the Reagan Revolution was kicked off when the president ordered the firing of 11,000 air traffic controllers for illegally striking for better working conditions.

We are currently experiencing perhaps the last phase of the Reagan Revolution. To be more exact, the decades of a massive transfer of the tax burden from the rich to workers and the salaried middle class, combined with the acceleration of the permanent war economy to $1 trillion a year has produced a new fiscal crisis. As in the late 1970s and early 1980s, this has been achieved politically by a bipartisan effort: no major Democratic governor and few Democratic big-city mayors have refused to do their part in forcing workers to pay for budget shortfalls. From the Northeast Coast to California, state and local governments have reduced teaching staffs, and when federal stimulus money was stopped, the burst of construction of the past two years rapidly came to an end. And with 15 million unemployed and at least 10 million underemployed, Democrats from Obama on down, with very few exceptions, have chanted the mantra of debt reduction, echoing the same Herbert Clark Hoover who brought FDR to the White House. The few remaining liberal and left voices, notably Nobel Laureates Joseph Stiglitz and Paul Krugman, have been crying in the wilderness, sidelined when not silenced.

As the early-twenty-first-century fiscal crisis gathered steam, most unions adopted two tactics to combat budget reductions and consequent layoffs. They sent teams of lobbyists—mostly activists and union staffers—to state capitols to convince legislators to increase taxes at the top of the economic pyramid or else to soften the layoff blow by economizing services. When this appeal fell flat, they offered concessions to prevent layoffs. A few held rallies involving hundreds of their members to protest the cuts. But around the country, almost nobody proposed or planned for the kind of action that happened in Madison.

The Madison protests of March and April 2011 bubbled from the base of the area's public employee unions. Tens of thousands marched, occupied the capitol, walked out of their classrooms and other public workplaces. But the huge outpouring cannot entirely be explained by Governor Walker's outrageous proposal or the smug arrogance of his administration. After all, Indiana's right-wing governor, Mitch Daniels, had already abolished collective bargaining for public employees and unions there had responded with less-than-ringing replies. And although the Democrats in the statehouses in Albany, New York and Sacramento, California would not go so far as to frontally assault their own political base, they, too, have drawn their playbook from the fiscal crisis of the 1980s. They have been willing to bargain over concessions rather than imposing them unless, of course, the workers and their unions become uppity, in which case, both governors announced, they will be forced to make cuts without the unions' cooperation.

In the heat of the 2011 demonstrations, Jim Cavanaugh, president of the Madison-area AFL-CIO council, had publicly entertained the possibility that the union's 94 affiliates would undertake a general strike, and the unions voted to authorize one. But when the recall effort intervened, Cavanaugh not only put the strike on hold, he also dissolved the committee formed to implement the resolution. For a while pockets of labor action and popular resistance remained, but once again, the idea of continuous and expanded direct action had been shelved in favor of electoral remedies.

Yet the outpouring of demonstrators in March and April was a sign that many rank-and-file unionists, students and community activists were tired of relying on the electoral system to address their demands. Why, then, when even Democratic state senators fled the capitol in order to deprive the governor and his allies of the quorum needed to pass the draconian bill, and the state Democratic Party came out in support of the public employees, did organized labor abandon the picket lines for the ballot box? It has been seventy years since most unions have been willing to assert their independence from the political system and engage in important direct action, such as an extralegal strike. Moreover, the unions in both the private and the public sectors have not seen themselves as part of a systemic opposition to the prevailing order. That the goal of the vast mobilization in Wisconsin was simply to protect collective bargaining beyond wages is a compelling illustration of how modest organized labor's demands have become.

During the two periods of twentieth-century labor upsurge, collective bargaining was achieved, initially, through worker disruption. This direct action was followed by legislation giving workers the opportunity to vote in state-supervised Labor Board elections for bargaining rights. But it was the employers who demanded and eventually benefited from the establishment of an electoral road to union recognition: in time, union leaders came to rely less and less on members' power and more and more on the law, and made steep compromises in order to retain the right to bargain. The real story of the past seventy-five years of labor's journey is the successful subordination of unions. The union contract is a legal vise; the law that is supposedly the worker's weapon is in fact a double-edged sword. When unions agree to long-term contracts of as much as six years, they are prohibited from striking for the length of the agreement. For the modest gains unions have made in legal guarantees, they have been obliged to surrender important rights. Labor law obliges a union to enforce its contract against illegal worker insurgencies, and in some states penalties are fairly stiff if union leaders sanction such actions. The law once helped unions to grow their membership, but after years of relentless and relatively successful right-wing attacks on workers' rights, some unionists have come to realize that the Labor Relations laws at the federal and local levels are mostly rigged against labor. In the 1980s, AFL-CIO president Lane Kirkland proposed the repeal of the National Labor Relations Act, because it had become so watered-down, it no longer served workers' interests.[2] Yet this idea has not been introduced into the dominant vocabulary of union discourse; far from fighting to repeal the law, union leadership is reluctant to challenge or even strategically evade it. Labor remains committed to "reforming" it. But the sorry history of forty years of that effort attests to its futility, even in states where Democrats have had legislative majorities.

Wisconsin has proven to be only a partial exception to the rule. When the insurgency grew, official labor bodies supported it, including national unions whose affiliates in Madison had decided to join, and sometimes lead, the protests. But since the national leaders are tied to the Democratic party and its national administration, it is no surprise that they have not called for parallel actions in other state capitols, especially those where Democrats occupy the governor's chair and control the legislature. Official labor can muster only shreds of opposition to the growing tendency toward legal restriction of labor's autonomy, aggravated by severe budget cuts when Republicans are in power. Wisconsin was an exception; in Ohio and Indiana the scope of the protest was much smaller. Even in Wisconsin, despite the concurrent example of the struggle in Egypt, labor's leadership could not imagine fighting until they won, fighting with tactics that could be interpreted as "permanent" actions until the legislation attacking the workers was rescinded.

Of course, Governor Walker's victory against collective bargaining should be seen from two viewpoints. On the one hand, when labor is loyal to the law under such circumstances and continues to believe that political action is its best course, unless it can decisively win a recall movement, it will end by falling back into line, as the unions did in Indiana. On the other hand, there is a chance that elements of the huge protest that began in Madison will engender new currents within the labor movement, revive the demand for direct action, inspire confrontation with the law through acts of civil disobedience—a time-honored strategy of the labor and civil rights movements. As the French sociologist and philosopher Henri Lefebvre once quipped, "events belie forecasts," and it is hard to predict such an eventuality. Some seeds have been planted, and it remains to be seen whether they will flower.[3]

Madison indicated the possible beginnings of a different labor movement. If such a movement emerges, it is certain to manifest itself first at the local level. Wisconsin was a likely cradle, because among its distinctive features is a student movement that has lasted for half a century, and many of its activists over those years have chosen to enter the labor movement rather than the professions. In the late 1960s, the Madison campus of the state university witnessed the formation of the first graduate student teaching assistants' union in the country, the Teaching Assistants' Association (TAA). Former state AFL-CIO president David Newby, who was a prominent organizer of the TAA, once said that the right would have to be bold to move decisively against unions in Wisconsin; if they could defeat labor there, they could likely do it anywhere. But as events unfolded, it was clear that the risk for antiunion forces was as great as the opportunity. There is a tradition of protest in Madison that may prove hard to eradicate.[4]

Wisconsin is also famous for its third-party movements. Even if the recall effort had been completely successful, it might not have put labor in a much better position than before—neither of the mainstream parties has shown much interest in alleviating the plight of public-sector workers. Will there now be a breakaway movement toward the formation of new progressive and labor parties at the state and local levels?

But it would be shortsighted to count on a new labor movement emerging within the confines of the existing unions. Throughout the country, new organizations are struggling to survive. Some of these are workers' centers; others are unions formed, especially by the working poor, without early prospects for achieving collective bargaining. The New York Taxi Workers Alliance, with about 15,000 members, relies almost exclusively on brief strikes, highway blockages, and city hall demonstrations to win its demands. The members negotiate informally with the city's Taxi and Limousine Commission. The workers' centers mobilize strikes, but not for the purpose of gaining union recognition, which, especially in manufacturing sectors, could result in capital flight. What they usually want is unpaid back wages, better safety conditions, and reinstatement of workers who have been fired for union activity.

The AFL-CIO has about the same proportion of private-sector members as unions did in 1931, and thanks to layoffs, the public-employee unions are declining rapidly, although they still retain enormous numbers. But it is worth remembering that before 1960 the public workers' unions were considered marginal by both the government and the mainstream unions. In the 1930s a variety of independent unions were formed without the blessing of the AFL, some under radical auspices. These unions were mostly weak, but they did engage in various forms of labor activity and several became the core organizations for future CIO affiliates. If current trends continue, it is conceivable that new outsider movements will arise in a similar fashion, especially among the working poor and professionals not covered by the teacher's unions. I believe that these movements could be the condition for the general revival of the labor movement, which for so many years has shown only a remarkable capacity for retreat.

A Season of Insurgency

The brief moment of direct action in the United States was not all that happened in 2011, of course. Tunisia's launch of the now legendary Arab Spring was quickly followed by continuous demonstrations and disruptions in Egypt. President Zine el-Abidine Ben Ali, autocrat of Tunisia for twenty-four years, and Egypt's thirty-year dictator, President Hosni Mubarak, were both forced to resign.

Egypt's revolution cut across class lines, though each class had its own agenda. The entrepreneurial and salaried (or professional) middle class wanted to establish a liberal-democratic regime; some of them favored dismantling of the country's nationalized enterprises and returning them to private hands. The military initially promised not to use the insurgency to install itself in power, then reneged and began a crackdown on the street protests. The long-suffering working class wanted to better their abysmal low wages and onerous working and living conditions, which were more typical of the nineteenth century than the twenty-first. As the liberal-democratic movement wound down, workers seized the opportunity and launched a series of strikes for trade-union rights and improved conditions. Their demands were greeted with scorn by some liberals and suppressed by military violence. But the struggle continues, and at the time of writing, in the post-Morsi era of autumn 2013, its outcome remains uncertain.

The popular upheavals in Tunisia and Egypt were followed by a rebellion in Libya against the Qaddafi regime—an uprising encouraged and supported militarily by NATO, which engaged in extensive bombing of government facilities, provided arms to the rebels, and under U.S. State Department tutelage conferred diplomatic legitimacy on the post-Qaddafi transitional council. Qaddafi himself was assassinated.

The Arab Spring was a complex event. On the one hand, it signaled popular determination to achieve emancipation from oppressive regimes. On the other, it has raised serious questions as to whether its outcome will be truly democratic. The new and more radical popular forces will need to overcome the repressive violence perpetrated by the military, and even if they do, the United States and NATO may manipulate the uprisings to install and reinforce their own version of modern capitalism, led by oil and other business interests, and permit or even encourage the newly founded states to suppress their labor and peasant movements. Or as the August 2013 overthrow of democratically elected President Morsi indicated, the ultimate beneficiaries of the revolution may be the military, which will use violence to control further street protests.

And what was the follow-up of the Madison Spring? Autumn 2011 proved that Wisconsin's demonstrators were not anomalies in an otherwise quiescent American population. On September 17, 2011, a small band of protesters occupied Zucotti Park, a privately owned sliver of land along New York City's Broadway, just north of Wall Street. When the media asked what were their demands, they responded generally that they demanded a better life, relief from the decline in living standards experienced by 99 percent of the population at the hands of the 1 percent who owned more than 40 percent of the country's wealth. Individuals said they were seeking jobs, alleviation of crushing student debt, better housing, and some even spoke of the imperative of ending American wars abroad. But the collective gathered in the park refused to offer specific policy demands, a decision that reflected both their strategy of avoiding political co-option and their alienation from the prevailing economic and political system. Clearly, having experienced a lifetime of betrayal, and resisting entreaties from some of their supporters to enter the existing electoral discourse, the occupiers were not seeking redress within the existing framework for reform.

Within a few weeks, no fewer than 110 occupations were reported throughout the United States and Canada, and soon the Occupy movement had spread to smaller towns not only within the United States but also around the globe. In many places the protesters received union support, notably from the Service Employees and the West Coast Longshore Workers; one New York march attracted 20,000 participants, many of them from unions. At first, the media, pundits, and politicians scoffed that the occupiers were nothing more than a small group of disconsolate hippies and youth who resented their own failures or, worse, were playing at disruption. But as the movement spread and deepened its base to include many older people who were unemployed and had little or no prospect of paid work, the media's tone became markedly different. For the right, the movement became worthy of serious attack, and the creepy shadow of red-baiting darkened some of their newspapers and airwaves. More centrist and liberal thinkers, including the *New York Times*, MSNBC, President Obama, and some Democratic politicians expressed sympathy for the movement and tried to integrate its message into their own agenda, particularly the proposal to address America's ills by modestly taxing the rich. Pro-Democratic websites like MoveOn.org, which had played an important role in the 2008 Obama victory, openly identified with the occupiers, but not with their "postpolitical" declarations.

I will discuss the Occupy movement in more detail later in this book. For now, it is important to understand that it was a labor movement of a new type—a class fight—and that a large number of its constituents were declassed intellectual workers and professionals who had studied for years to obtain an advanced degree, then graduated from university only to discover there were no jobs, that at best they could work in various service occupations such as those in the food industry, where employment is precarious and often part-time, and its rewards uneven. Notably, they imaginatively mounted their protest by dwelling in public spaces, rather than temporarily demonstrating in or in front of them or mass–marching through them. Their governance of these occupied spaces was based on the tradition of popular assemblies associated with historical movements like the Paris Commune, New England town meetings, and the workers' councils of the post–World War I European revolutions, and their commitment to them was total. In contrast, except for the West Coast Longshore Workers unions that supported Occupy limited themselves to weekend demonstrations that did not disrupt the normal workweek or violate their no-strike contracts. Nevertheless, it is important that a portion of local labor unions and the top leaders of the AFL-CIO made appearances at rallies held at Occupy sites.

That first year, as winter approached, people questioned how long the occupations in New York; Boston; Philadelphia; Washington, D.C.; Oakland, California; Portland, Oregon; and Midwestern cities such as Chicago and Detroit were going to last as the weather grew colder. By November, a coordinated effort by eighteen big-city mayors, Democrats and Republicans, had forced the occupiers to disband, sometimes by violent means, except in a few cities such as Los Angeles and Philadelphia where the local political establishment feared a blowback. Perhaps the most revealing official reaction was that of Oakland's ostensibly progressive mayor, who called out riot police to disperse the occupiers. Yet though their staying power had been questioned, and their occupations forcibly brought to an end, the occupiers had captured the attention of the world. *Time* magazine awarded its 2011 Person of the Year cover to The Protester, a tribute shared by Occupy Wall Street and the Arab Spring.

Economy as a Dependent Variable: Politics Takes Command

In the course of this book, I will consistently argue, against widespread belief and opinion, that although important in political terms, the economy is a dependent variable in the structure of political and social life. The worldwide Occupy movement began on Wall Street as a protest against the richest 1 percent of the U.S. population and one of the issues it focused on was the growing joblessness among its mainly middle-class members. Most of the occupiers of Zucotti Park were either college students or college graduates; some were unemployed technical and professional workers. And the main rallying cry of the protest, that 99 percent of the population were bereft of support as a tiny minority accumulated vast wealth, seemed to validate the idea that the economy is always *the* issue. Yet the protest was directed as much at government as it was at big banks and big investors. Indeed, in many cities, occupiers squatted in or adjacent to city hall parks. That the state plays a vital role in the economy is an indisputable proposition among the general population as much as it is in expert opinion. When economic failure looms, the large banks, insurance companies, and goods-production corporations turn to the state, and not only during the latest depression. When joblessness rises to alarming proportions, the public turns its ire, in the first place, on the national government, which it expects should alleviate their suffering as well as that of their employers.

State intervention in times of financial crisis was not initiated by the New Deal. It has been a practice for as long as capitalism has been the reigning system. And the state has often paid for its bailout of large companies and financial institutions by imposing the costs on working- and middle-class people. Such a "bailout" is a politically legitimated transfer of wealth from the majority to a tiny minority based on the fallacious assumption that big corporate interests are at the heart of job creation and economic stability. Production, distribution, and consumption are entwined with actions of the state not only through regulation but also by this proclivity of governments to rescue the largest banks and industrial corporations in times of crisis. At least since World War II, this has partly been accomplished through the awarding of a huge volume of government-funded war and education contracts; the building of federal highways, which have become vital means of commercial transportation, and of recreational facilities; and the enormous expansion of public employment. Until the recent austerity measures insisted on by business interests and dutifully imposed by federal, state, and local governments, public employment was, for thirty years, effectively the only major growth sector for decent-paying jobs. Meanwhile, for more than a decade, private-sector service "jobs" have enlarged the size of the precarious strata of the working class: hospitality, tourism, and retail produce work that is almost all low-wage and offers no health care or other benefits. Moreover, a good number of these jobs are contingent—some seasonal, others dependent for their existence on the vicissitudes of the wholesale and retail markets. The nature of economic activity is closely linked to the cultural presuppositions that permeate everyday life. As Marx and Engels have argued:

> According to the materialist conception of history, the ultimately determining element in history is the production and reproduction of real life. More than this neither Marx nor I have ever asserted. Hence if somebody twists this into saying that the economic element is the only determining one, he transforms that proposition into a meaningless abstract,

senseless phrase. The economic situation is the basis, but the various elements of the superstructure—political forms of the class struggle and its results, to wit: constitutions, established forms, and even reflexes of these actual struggles in the brains of the participants; political, juristic, philosophical theories; religious views and their further development into systems of dogma—also exercise their influence upon the course of the historical struggles *and in many cases preponderate in determining their form* [emphasis mine].[5]

We must remember that our needs are *historically conditioned* as well as biological. What we consider absolute necessity depends a great deal on how much disposable income we possess, and also on what we consider an appropriate living standard. We expect to live in a manner that corresponds to the historical level of material culture. For example, ownership of a single-household home does more than fulfill our need to have a roof over our heads. It has become a measure of the Good Life for most Americans, except for a segment of the very rich who gravitate toward luxury apartments in the major cities, and professionals, who often prefer a cosmopolitan lifestyle to suburban sprawl. When blue-collar and even salaried white-collar workers discover that they are unable to afford a home or to maintain the one they have, they and their families and communities often experience a cultural shock.

Another example: as a mark of *measurement,* it has become an entirely rational economic calculation to send our children to an institution of postsecondary education. College enrollment serves as a sign of *cultural achievement.* And finally, there is the everyday cultural presupposition that we will and should raise our material *status.* For instance, our automobiles have become more than a practical convenience in a country with relatively spotty mass public transportation; they are also a mark of our personal standing and style. Those who drive five-, ten- or fifteen-year-old cars are regarded as eccentric, poor, or seriously out of fashion.[6] For this reason, it is not uncommon for people of modest means to drive late-model cars that soak up a significant portion of their monthly income.

An economic crisis can put intolerable pressures on these needs. Meanwhile, there is little agreement about what we mean by "the economy." The ambiguity is referable first of all to the multiplicity of references "the economy" has. Business interests, including bankers, stockbrokers, and owners of industrial facilities, are mostly focused on their own profits to the virtual exclusion of everything else; small businesses in the service industries worry about consumption, a concern that that overlaps with the concerns of working people: consumption does not flourish when there are fewer full-time jobs and incomes are lower. Only economists seem to care about rates of economic growth, because most of them still believe that growth is the key to everything economic, including job creation. And there, we seem to be operating on over- or underestimated data, because the statistical methodology is flawed.

Nevertheless, policymakers as well as academic economists continue to think and act on these questionable assumptions. If the reported annual growth rate exceeds the expansion of the labor market, we are said to be in a recovery period or one of stability. "Labor productivity" is duly reported, but its significance or its content is rarely analyzed. Yet economists have been mystified by the persistent high levels of unemployment, because they have assumed that job creation is a function of overall economic growth and have either discounted or ignored the impact of capital flight, stagnant or falling wages, and particularly of technology, all of which challenge their traditional formulas.

Most economists have made only a meager contribution to our collective understanding of the significance of technology for the production of goods and services, including its effect on employment, let alone to a deeper understanding of what constitutes "labor productivity." Economic wisdom has failed to measure the impact of technological innovation on jobs by industry and occupation. William DiFazio and I argued twenty years ago on three major points concerning this:

1. Technological change refers, primarily, to the introduction of machinery and processes that reduce the proportion of direct labor in the production of commodities.[7]
2. Companies introduce new technologies to improve their bottom line; they increase their profit margin by reducing or eliminating their need for human labor, destroying jobs in order to save costs.

3. Few economists have bothered to assess the added impact of capital flight on jobs, wages, and consumption. In the main they have created or accepted the notion that recession and recovery are measured by macroeconomic growth rates, defined as the monetary value of aggregate goods and services, even if real wages and income decline and joblessness remains high.

There is also little clarity about the definition of a "job." With the exception of the small coterie who study income inequality, most economists in their concept of "jobs" fail to differentiate between skilled, unskilled and semiskilled jobs, or between the jobs that pay a living wage or salary and those that, increasingly, do not. In Europe, unemployment calculations include not only full-time joblessness but also the portion of part-time workers' time that is unemployed and unpaid. But in the United States, official labor statistics—generated largely by professional economists—give the same weight to part-time work as to a full-time job. Hence the disparity between official rates and actual rates; recently, however, some experts have begun to calculate the unfiled and unpaid hours of part-time workers seeking full-time jobs, raising the unemployment rate by more than 40 percent. After the crash of 2007–08, the official unemployment rate climbed to 9 percent, 14 million workers. But if discouraged workers who have stopped seeking employment and part-timers who would accept a full-time job are added to the calculation, the figure climbs to 23 million, more than 15 percent.

So, when the Department of Labor releases employment figures, their predictions of an uptick are often erroneous, because wage stagnation and the growth of contingent and part-time work reduce the income and creditworthiness of a growing sector of the "employed" workforce. Without credit, one can't buy most durable goods—homes, cars, furniture—or obtain a loan to pay for college or professional or vocational school tuition.

Thus "the economy" has a multitude of references: Do we mean the profits of capital? The level of wages, employment, and unemployment? Gross domestic product? Consumer spending? The income gap between the very rich and the rest of us? The costs to capital of doing business?

General living standards? All of the above? What role does the car culture play in determining economic structure; what is the impact of rapid suburbanization of the majority of the population in the postwar period, or the preponderance of families in single-household homes rather than apartments? What is the price of the expansion of the politically wrought social welfare state? And what is the impact of the racial divide, which has both economic and ideological dimensions? If a huge number of blacks and Latinos suffer poverty at its officially defined level (which is ridiculously understated), or are within the actual, realistic range of poverty, what effect does this have on the capacity of the economy to achieve growth? And if the current social and economic arrangements have consigned a substantial minority of the population to permanent unemployment, what does that do to the claim that America is a democratic society?

And an attempt to define *economy* raises other ambiguities. If we return to the classical definition, developed by Thomas Hobbes, Adam Smith, William Petty and David Ricardo, we notice a modifier, *political*. When they spoke of "political economy," these founders did not refer exclusively—or even principally—to the relationship of labor and commodity markets to the state. By "political" they meant the terms under which the production, distribution, and consumption of goods and services takes place and, more specifically, the share of the social product that accrues respectively to labor, capital, and agricultural interests. They recognized, sometimes explicitly and often tacitly, that in the capitalist epoch the shares of the different actors are structurally unequal. At the same time, Smith and Ricardo argued for the doctrine that labor is paid according to its time spent in making goods and that the wages of capital are compensation for risk-taking and advancing the means by which labor is employed. For this reason, they explained, profits are a function of the market, external to the labor process itself.

Marx's critique of classical political economy stated that the worker produces both her wages and a surplus that is transformed into capital (profits). Marx argued that profits derive from the surplus created by workers in the time after the time they spend reproducing their own labor power, that is, their ability to return to work the next day. Workers' wages, therefore, represent only a portion of the working day; the surplus value from which profits accrue is extracted from the unpaid portion of that working day. A failure or refusal to recognize this spawned the fiction that capital creates wealth, a tale that continues to hold sway today. For example, conservatives in both leading political parties in the United States insist that tax policy should reflect the taken-for-granted assumption that the wealthy are both wealth and job creators rather than the beneficiaries of ownership of productive property and should therefore be taxed at a lower rate than the general population. Our tax code reflects this doctrine. For example, hedge fund managers pay a low tax rate based on the fiction that because their income yields capital gains they therefore contribute to the national economic growth. The two parties differ on the vague concept of equality of sacrifice: Democrats believe that high earners should be granted tax concessions for hiring workers in times of recession but should also pay an enhanced share of the national debt. Still, they are like Republicans in equating the economy with the total society.

The economy is only one aspect of a social totality that consists of economic, political, sociocultural, and ideological relationships that are closely interconnected. Moreover, which sphere will shape the course of social life is not determined *in advance,* but instead depends on specific historical conditions. The economy itself might, under certain circumstances, be derivative of other influences, especially politics and culture. That the state has always been an important component in economic relations should be self-evident, but ideologues persist in describing the contemporary capitalist system in terms of the "free" market (to paraphrase A. J. Liebling, who further noted that the press is free for those who own one). They ignore the production sphere. Proponents of the idea of market capitalism also conveniently ignore the many functions performed by the state and federal governments in almost every aspect of the economy, from job creation within the state bureaucracy, to subsidies to banks, manufacturers, and incomes of individuals, to the provision of infrastructure. We will enumerate these interventions below, but for the present it is useful to recall how much of tax revenues are devoted to providing the infrastructure without which economic activity as we know it would surely grind to a halt, or how crucial public sector jobs are for the maintenance and growth of consumption. In short, the idea that the economy is relatively independent and the chief determinant of social relations requires amendment, if not complete revision.

And taken together, these examples suggest that in the course of social life, even economic phenomena are in principle unpredictable, because of the very complexity they purport to explain. More, economic predictions rarely anticipate sudden historical changes or the impact of political influences on economic currents. By "political" I do not refer exclusively to state decisions, but also to the politics of investment. That few economists anticipated the collapse of financial markets in 1987 or twenty years later in 2007, were able to analyze the forces configured by a combination of nefarious bank and state policies, is only one illustration of my point. The accumulation of hundreds of billions of dollars in bad securities drawn from irresponsible housing debt was by no means caused by "free" market failure, but by a series of tacit agreements between lax government regulators, the rating agency Standard & Poor's, and lending institutions that permitted many people to acquire mortgages without depositing equity; millions of borrowers were obliged to pay only the interest on the mortgage principle, for a limited time period. Needless to say, when the interest rates ballooned amid sharply declining housing prices, millions were forced into foreclosure, some lenders collapsed, and the banks and insurance companies turned to the federal government for a huge bailout, which, under Republican and Democratic administrations, they promptly received. The private sector had once again persuaded the government to save it on the backs of taxpayers and especially of wage-earners and professional and technical salaried employees.

Classical and neoclassical economic theories are based on an unquestioned belief in the sanctity of private property, derived from the notion that the accumulation of property, especially in its capital form, is tantamount to wages for the labor of enterprise, or entrepreneurship. Profits are the reward for private risk, initiative and investment. Yet there is overwhelming evidence that with only partial exceptions, such as the dot.com bubble, our social media and computer revolutions were developed from the ground up (although computer research and development was a wartime project of the federal government, like nuclear weapons and energy). Nevertheless, the largest and most powerful corporations, which effectively dominate our markets, are oligopolies, bureaucratic organizations in which creativity—technological or otherwise—plays a subordinate role. In fact, innovations that threaten profits or hierarchical power are frequently suppressed. Moreover, for more than a half-century the largest industrial corporations have depended on the federal government for a considerable portion of their revenue. Military contracts remain important for aircraft, electrical machinery, and other industrial businesses and, of course, physical, biological, chemical, and engineering research. Federal, state, and local governments also award contracts for a variety of public functions: construction of public buildings, and roads, corporate consulting to government agencies, privatized training, and educational goods and services such as textbooks, school equipment, and so forth. These contracts transfer hundreds of billions of dollars in payments from wage and salary earners to private-sector capital.

The current economic crisis, in contrast to the postwar recessions, has already lasted more than seven years and may be classified as a depression. Many Americans now realize that financialization has displaced industrial production as the heart of the United States economy. The Occupy Wall Street calculation was too generous: in fact, less than 0.1 percent of the population controls nearly 40 percent of all American wealth. But the financial sector, which has enjoyed the greatest part of this capital accumulation, produces relatively few jobs. As we learned from the bank and corporate failures of 2008–09, a large portion of capital relies on tax revenues derived from the rest of the population. These revenues are chiefly transferred to the banks through credit-card and student debt and through the massive stimulus packages awarded by federal and state governments. Since debt produces nothing but paper, capital may be said to rest on fiction—that is, on the promise of future redemption—rather than on real assets. And that the main banks and other lending institutions are permitted to withhold loans to small business, potential home owners, and some students and private individuals is a measure of the degree to which politics, not economics, has taken command. The ostensible purpose of the bailouts, to shore up the economy, is subverted by finance capital's refusal to help dispense the state's largesse to the underlying population, and the state refuses to take action to force it to do so.

Yet the public imagination sees the massive shift in the political economy since the 1970s as the result of "corporate greed" rather than of systemic transformations—as if the country's well-being could be restored if only the 1 percent who own huge wealth were properly disciplined. But who will perform the task of bringing them into line? The state is presumed to be a nonpartisan system of institutions subject to public sovereignty. If it were, electoral politics would be the proper vehicle for restraining the runaway corporate tycoons. Somehow the public sees the present time as a moment of economic determinism, and the ideological force of this notion is fed by the dominant media and discussions on the left.

The Concept of Economic Determinism

Economic determinism runs like a red thread throughout American history, but it attained unimpeachable prestige in the era of the Great Depression and has held pride of place in our political theory ever since. As an ideology, it forecloses thinking and becomes a system for effectively controlling dissent and discouraging practical transformative activity. The key idea of economic determinism is that all historical events, at least in the capitalist epoch, spring from the relation of actors to economic factors. In its crudest version, it insists that economic "interests" dictate political decisions. Thus, in the current conversation, populists and even many progressives deplore corporate greed as the source of our economic woes. Those arguing on a slightly more elevated level say that actors on all sides are motivated by pecuniary self-interest. According to this view, a professed concern for the national interest is always a mask concealing conscious or even unconscious concern for particular gains. At the pinnacle of the hierarchy of economic determinism doctrines stand those that attribute political decisions to underlying economic considerations, but not necessarily those motivated by greed.

For instance, if the jobs picture is lousy, government is forced to find ways to intervene, although the form of intervention may vary according to different politicians' conceptions of causes and effects. Contemporary conservatives argue that since the private sector provides most jobs, imposing higher taxes on rich individuals and corporations is self-defeating. The diminishing corps of Keynesians, on the other hand, long ago lost faith in the inclination of the wealthiest to create jobs, at least good jobs at home—they are more likely to create them offshore, in the lowest-wage countries with the fewest workplace regulations. Therefore, liberals say, the government should raise revenues by taxing the rich and using the money to create jobs or provide income to the long-term unemployed. Keynesian and neoconservative prescriptions for recovery and who should pay for it are obviously widely different, but both sides agree that the key political question is the state of the economy.

The concept of economic determinism has a deep and extensive intellectual background. Among its fullest American expressions is Charles Beard's influential *An Economic Interpretation of the Constitution of the United States* (1913). In this work, Beard demonstrates that many of those who attended the Constitutional Convention, including the leading framers of the document, had a direct self-interest in the provisions that were finally enacted. Beard was incorrectly charged with being a Marxist; more accurately, he was a progressive Jeffersonian who believed that political actors are mainly motivated by economic interests. His views are far more consistent with the current populist belief that many of our troubles stem from corporate greed than with the theory of the historical materialists that they are inherent in capitalism per se. Beard saw that the nineteenth and early twentieth centuries were marked by an inordinate concentration of economic power by the largest corporations, and he concluded that this had resulted in distortions of American democracy.

Beard influenced an entire generation of scholars and political activists as well as many socialists and laborites for whom economic determinism was self-evident. His work helped them throw aside the "great man" theory—the idea that history is made by its George Washingtons, Napoleons, Lincolns, Roosevelts, and Hitlers. In 1927, Beard and his wife,

Mary, published their magnum opus, *The Rise of American Civilization*. As with his earlier study, its main thesis is that economic self-interest results in the concentration of wealth, which inevitably leads to powerful political interventions by the trusts and monopolistic corporations. Democracy is held hostage by them, regardless of which of the two main political parties is in power or what leaders are elected.

This theory gains an even sharper point now that the Supreme Court has ruled that it is illegal to limit the size of corporate campaign contributions, but in fact big business has always found a way to work its will on the political process. Its huge influence was already in evidence during the post–Civil War years, and it increased throughout the twentieth century. Even when regulatory legislation tried to restrict wealth concentration, rich corporations and individuals always had plenty of money to corrupt politicians through campaign contributions and other pecuniary sweeteners.[8]

The Beards' book became an important intellectual guide for the trust-busters of the New Deal, particularly Thurman Arnold, who directed investigations and prosecutions of some of the more flagrant violators of the Sherman Anti-Trust legislation of 1892 and its update in 1913, the Clayton Act. Wisconsin Senator Robert La Follette conducted a celebrated series of hearings and studies during the mid-1930s, under the aegis of the Temporary National Economic Committee (TNEC), that exposed the extent of wealth concentration. When FDR was prevented from expanding the Supreme Court in order to establish the legality of some of his key reforms, which had been rejected by the "nine old men," he lashed out against the "economic royalists" who, he claimed, were subverting the political system. But after World War II, as the economy expanded at a relatively swift pace, Congress and state legislatures were predisposed to accept the interventions of big business and its lobbies as the price the country must pay for its unparalleled prosperity. The historical antipathy of the general population toward the very rich was partially mollified by philanthropists, like the steel mogul Andrew Carnegie and the Rockefellers, and by a visible enlightened segment of the ruling corporate elite, notably Gerard Swope of General Electric, who vocally supported social reform, including the right of workers to organize unions.[9]

Our current general economic crisis at a time of very concentrated wealth and extreme income inequality has its own peculiar features, but in broad outline it is by no means new. Such crises have afflicted all levels of our government for centuries. During our nineteenth century's Gilded Age, the emerging trusts exercised an almost unchallenged rule over the private-sector workplace and government at all levels. The labor movement then—both unions and radicals—was very weak, and it was relatively easy for ruling elites to address a crisis by shifting its burden onto workers and local communities.

There were, of course, some real struggles to break the success of these relentless capitalist offensives: the great rail strikes of 1877, 1884, and 1894; the Homestead Steel Strike of 1892; turn-of-the-century coal- and copper-mining struggles; and, in 1886, the beginning of labor's half-century fight for the eight-hour day—a revolutionary concept at a time when the workday ranged from ten to fourteen hours. Unions also fought for legislation against child labor and (egregiously) against women's right to work nights and operate some machinery. Many of these battles were lost, but they planted the seeds of a major reversal in the relationship of political and social forces between capital and labor. Meanwhile, their failure to pass and thus mitigate the extreme concentration of wealth and curb the reckless accumulation of further wealth set the stage for the crash of 1929 that launched the Great Depression.

In the teeth of that depression, the administration of Herbert Clark Hoover ran and operated on some of the same ideas that animate the current right, except that he made some modest moves toward federal intervention in stimulating economic activity. But even at a time when a third of the labor force was unemployed and a significant number hungry and homeless, believing that "prosperity is just around the corner" and that it would be immoral to coddle the nonworking poor, he refused to order either mass relief or a federally sponsored jobs program. That was left to his successful challenger in 1932, Franklin Delano Roosevelt.

Barack Obama in his 2008 campaign hinted, but did not promise, that he would follow the aggressive jobs program of FDR's New Deal. Four years later, having failed to do more than bail out the leading banks and industrial corporations, Obama ran for reelection with enthusiastic labor backing. And again the Obama campaign did not directly confront unemployment and precarity by promising jobs or any income beyond an extension of jobless benefits. Labor, after donating $400 million in union funds and a small army of volunteers, settled for little more in return than assurances that the administration would protect what workers had been given in the past—a vow that the workers could not entirely rely upon.

During the inconclusive budget negotiations of 2012–13, Obama offered a deal to his Republican adversaries. He would agree to certain deficit-reduction measures, including modified cost-of-living raises for Social Security recipients, further cuts in health care programs, and job cuts in the federal bureaucracy, if these cuts were accompanied by small tax increases on the very rich. He even changed his proposal from raising taxes on family incomes of $250,000 or more to raising them only on family incomes at or above $400,000. The GOP negotiators countered with a starting point of $1 million, and the deal fell apart.

In his State of the Union and Inaugural addresses in 2013, Obama promised no new major federal job-creating programs and did not discuss the indications of growing poverty among the long-term unemployed, nor did he propose a new incomes policy (which would include long-term unemployment insurance, guaranteed income, measures to enhance social security benefits, etcetera) or—despite his encouraging words about the need to revive American industrial production—articulate an industrial policy. He nibbled at the edges of the crisis but sounded no call that urgently addressed it or acknowledged its depth. And since there was no audible grumbling on the left, even from those within his own party, he escaped unscathed.

Today, nobody with the political authority to do it has matched the New Deal's inadequate but dramatic policy of creating jobs. We live in an era when mainstream politics is firmly in possession of the right. The best the liberals and their union allies can manage is to defend the tatters of welfare-state benefits enacted, most of them, more than seventy years ago. Part of the problem is the liberals' lack of imagination. But the real reason the right has been able to set the political agenda is perfectly expressed in William Butler Yeats' words: "The best lack all conviction while the worst are full of passionate intensity."

In a society controlled by the ideology of economic determinism, labor, and particularly the working poor, gets left behind, without any tools or institutions to fight back and catch up. Theorists use concepts such as "corporate greed" to account for wealth concentration, implying that in a well-run capitalist economy it would be possible to avoid the costs of capital accumulation and centralized ownership of finance and the material means of production. The unions refuse to address frequent economic crises and wealth inequality at the political level and engage in the search for societal alternatives, and so they and the workers they represent remain victims of a system that consistently betrays them. Progressives and the left are not prepared to systematically confront militarization in everyday life as well as in the workplace, or seriously challenge prevailing cultural beliefs—especially those that uphold the credit system and encourage patterns of oppressive consumption. These failures have crippled even the most militant sectors of the labor movement.

CHAPTER TWO

The Mass Psychology
of Liberalism

"Fear eats the soul."

—Ali, in *Ali, Angst essen Seele auf*, Rainer Maria Fassbinder (dir.)

The United States' privatized presidential contest is a brain-numbing two-year process, sport and spectacle alike. Immediately after the November 2010 midterm elections, Republican hopefuls hit the presidential starting gate, and the race was on. President Obama galloped around the country in reelection dress, assuring his listeners that the economic recovery, although slow, was progressing steadily, despite his failure to craft a jobs program for the 25 million still jobless and underemployed. We had sixteen months of ads, debates, scandals and wedge issues to get through before November 2012. Yet not even the fiercest of these could hide how little difference there is between Democratic and Republican ideologies. They are two traditional branches of liberalism.

Liberalism stands alongside economic determinism as the other ideological pillar that has propped up our country's social and political edifice, just as important historically and even more significant today. The mass psychology of liberalism has conditioned labor leaders, workers, and the working poor and unemployed to a passive cynicism and totally compromised relations with capital.

Liberalism is, in fact, the dominant capitalist ideology. But like most dominant ideologies it has several variants. The eighteenth-century doctrine rests on three concepts of freedom: freedom of the market from government regulation, that is, laissez-faire economics; freedom of the individual from coercion, a negative liberty from social laws or customs enforced by a central power; and freedom of association, the right of individuals to organize and assemble in groups and parties, and seek elective office under the capitalist state. Note that underlying all variants of liberalism is the proposition that capitalism is the unchangeable thing (as Hegel puts it), the framework within which all policy functions.

As Karl Polanyi demonstrates in *The Great Transformation*, the "free market" has never really existed. For centuries, business has sought and secured the financial, political, and legal support of the state but has resisted the state according the same privileges to the rest of us. Private capital avoids shouldering the risk of building roads, ports, post offices, power systems, waterworks, airports, or public transport. On the contrary, it relies on government to provide major transportation and communication media, law and civil courts, a police force, and emergency services; to zone land, issue currency, and set interest rates and monetary policy; and to regulate—and repress—labor. It is a measure of the degree to which the unions have been integrated into the liberal consensus that they have welcomed state regulation of labor relations and almost invariably pride themselves on their obedience to the laws, including the supposedly bilateral collective bargaining agreement. The no-strike provision of most labor contracts reveals the true character of labor law.

Labor law is, in brief, an invocation to class collaboration, or at least class peace. It has above all a regulatory function, which is hidden under its apparent declaration of the rights of labor. If this characterization appears unduly harsh, recall the Supreme Court's many employer-friendly amendments to the Labor Relations Act even before the Taft-Hartley amendments of 1947, of which more later. Section 8 of the Labor Relations Act granted employers free speech rights that effectually legalized tactics designed to intimidate workers during union representation election campaigns. These rights were not a major factor in union representation elections until the late 1940s. Since then, first in the South and then almost everywhere in the country, employer intimidation of workers became a routine feature of these elections

Nor is the creation of commercially useful physical and social public infrastructure or the creation, enforcement, and upholding of business-friendly laws the only assistance that capital receives from the organs of the state. When everything blows up, as it inevitably does, from financial markets and foreign relations to oil spills and leaks from nuclear reactors, government assumes the liabilities, cleans up the mess, and restores the profit-making order. We have seen the oil and mining corporations' flagrant denial of responsibility for oil spills, fatal mining accidents, and widespread pollution in mining regions, and General Electric's and upstate New York paper companies' decades of failure to address the pollution in the Hudson River.[1]

It is ironical that in recent decades, these free market liberals have been labeled conservatives, even though they are no longer conservationists, as were their Republican predecessors. They insist against all logic and science that either climate change is nothing new, or that it does not exist, or that even if it does, the market will somehow take care of it. Environmental policing is one responsibility they are not eager to hand over to the state, and they oppose regulations aimed even at slowing down, never mind reversing, the coming disaster. This is not conservatism in any logical definition of the word, but it is a logical adherence to classic laissez-faire capitalism.

The second type of American liberalism has developed some ideas beyond those of the eighteenth century; this is modern liberalism, or progressivism. It began to take shape in the post–Civil War era, advocating government protection for small business during the rise of the giant trusts, and for a central bank, which led to the creation of the Federal Reserve Bank in 1913. Progressives also responded to Upton Sinclair's exposé of the meatpacking industry, *The Jungle*, in 1905, the mass protest by New York City garment workers in 1909, and the 1911 Triangle Shirtwaist Factory fire in Lower Manhattan by enacting federal and local laws regulating workplace and consumer goods safety, and also raising building standards for the notoriously hazardous tenement housing where many workers lived.

It is important to realize that in advocating and enacting these reforms progressives have demonstrated no substantive disagreement with the free market, freedom of association, and freedom from coercion as the pillars of our political and economic ideology. The underlying premise of modern liberalism is that in a free market society, the least powerful members—small business owners, rank-and-file workers, women, and racial and other minorities—will need some protection from uncontrolled market forces. But under no circumstance, except perhaps during severe economic crisis or in wartime, do they believe that the state should own or operate productive property. The New Deal reforms—Social Security, the National Labor Relations Act, unemployment and workers' compensation, the minimum wage and the forty-hour week—represent the apex of modern social reform. Further achievements followed—Medicare, Medicaid, the Civil and Voting Rights Acts, and the regulatory burst under Nixon—but since the 1970s the signal activity of modern liberalism, incremental change, has ground to a halt.

The age of real labor reform ended in 1938, but liberal reformism remains the leading edge of a dubious left in American politics: dubious because the mainstream left does not oppose the capitalist system (except rhetorically), holding that capitalism can be sufficiently reformed to secure a measure of social justice. This assumption was forged during the rise of mass industrial unionism in the 1930s and it once had considerable validity. But since 1938, workers have won only a single major systemic victory: the enactment of Medicare and Medicaid in 1965. Voting rights and civil rights were achieved by a massive black freedom movement and its white allies. Three liberal national governments—Roosevelt's, Truman's, and Kennedy's—opposed them. By 1964, lunch counter sit-ins, the Montgomery bus boycott, the 1963 March on Washington for Jobs and Freedom and the fateful demonstrations in Birmingham, which were met with brutal police violence, posed a sufficient threat to liberal hegemony that President Lyndon Johnson finally conceded—a capitulation that cost the Democrats their once solid base in the South.

In 1973, through a Supreme Court decision rather than action from a Congress in the thrall of conventional religious morality, women won the right to legal abortion, which they have been forced to constantly defend ever since. Except for the embattled *Roe v. Wade*, the past forty-five years have been a time of retreat from the struggle for popular reform. The liberal organizations, the unions, and the liberal organs of opinion have confined their activities and appeals to defending the gains of the past and have proposed few, if any, actions for new ones.

Within this context, it is fair to say that since the 1930s the battalions of the American left, organized mainly in and around the Communist and Socialist parties and some social democratic-oriented industrial unions, might better be described as "left-liberal." Multiple factors determined their migration from revolution to reform, but perhaps the main reason was the precipitous rise of fascism in Italy and, especially, in Germany. To defend representative democratic institutions, the Communists and a substantial fraction of erstwhile Socialists sought not only to unify the left but also, crucially, to seek alliances with the liberals, including a sector of "progressive" capitalists. Since then, with few exceptions, they have refused to publicly discuss, let alone agitate for, alternative economic systems such as socialism and communism. Even most of the so-called revolutionary socialist parties and formations have confined their activities to economic struggles within trade unions; austerity fight-backs; organized opposition to U.S. imperialism and racism; and the defense of abortion rights and civil liberties. They also make some effort to advance left-wing ideas: a smattering of institutions offer a socialist education, notably New York's Brecht Forum, and in academia and among college-educated professional activists study groups have mushroomed, mainly to read Marx's *Capital* and Lenin's *State and Revolution* and *Imperialism: The Highest Stage of Capitalism*.

If since the rise of fascism the American left has been in retreat, since the crushing of German liberal-democratic institutions in the early 1930s the liberal center has been in a state of perpetual panic. True, it has defended the reforms enacted under the second New Deal, which were really a response to, and achievement of, the working-class uprisings from 1933 to 1937. But on more than one occasion these liberals have been willing to enter into compromises with conservatives in the hopes of thwarting the more bellicose right. Further, the bulk of progressive institutions and intellectuals capitulated completely to the Cold War and to aggressive U.S. foreign policy in the 1990s and the first decade of the twenty-first century. This capitulation helped stymie any hope of reform, though its influence has been largely denied by the liberal center, which until the 1980s insisted on the compatibility of "guns and butter."

And the last thirty years have introduced a new constraint: the right's prolonged antilabor and antipopular offensive, which has effectively eroded, and in some respects, seriously eroded the social welfare state. Capital and its political and ideological supporters have succeeded in painting the social wage as theft by theft: the shiftless poor, thereby stealing from the decent citizens who pay oppressive taxes to support them. Carefully avoiding a direct assault on old-age pensions (that is, Social Security) or unemployment compensation per se, the right has focused its attack on the only guaranteed-income program in American history: welfare, or aid to the long-term unemployed and a portion of the working poor. Although liberals have been inclined to reject the ideology—that the poor are undeserving—they have not strongly resisted the offensive itself. In 1996, Congress passed the Republican-sponsored Personal Responsibility and Work Opportunity Act, which rescinded the guaranteed income, required welfare recipients to work at dead-end jobs in order to receive checks, and limited coverage to five years. The centrist-liberal President Bill Clinton signed it, and fearful of a Republican victory in the presidential election that year, the liberals, most of the left, and the unions did not protest.

What is lacking is any public perspective beyond liberal reformism. Sharing the liberal aversion to new thinking, the self-designated left has spurned utopianism, and without that vision radicalism is only a series of anticapitalist rants. The American left, sadly following the pattern most of the European left, is a party of *protest and resistance*. We are in a historical moment of one-dimensionality. The major distinctions between the liberals and the left are purely tactical: the liberals are devoted to working within the system, but have lost their taste for even incremental change; the left proclaims that the system is essentially rotten, but seems to have lost its taste for devising and articulating alternatives to the rotten system they oppose. Thus they race from struggle to struggle and, with numbing regularity lose, witnessing the disintegration of their movement and/or its co-option by elements of the modern liberal center.

Fear Eats the Soul

L iberals today are in the grip of a great fear—the fear of losing their comfortable berths in the professions, the unions, and the universities. Some activists of yesteryear have gone over to the enemy, but the larger number have simply gone into a more or less invisible political retirement. Among those who have not, that fear has produced considerable bad faith: at some level liberals know better, but manage to convince themselves of positions that contradict their beliefs. Some actually hailed Bill Clinton's capitulation to welfare reform as a valid move toward making the poor more self-reliant. Liberalism's dedication to social reform has declined into nostalgia. They still wear the mantle of the New Deal, but have little political will to fight for its unfulfilled promises. Most liberals inside and outside Congress signed on to Barack Obama's Affordable Care Act, a huge gift to private insurance corporations, as it requires almost everyone to purchase health insurance without specifying what price can be called affordable, instead of insisting on a national single-payer plan that would have largely put for-profit health insurers out of business. Most liberals supported Obama's snail's-pace schedule for withdrawing troops from Iraq and Afghanistan, which allowed private military companies plenty of time to pick up the slack of the occupation. The withdrawal will not end U.S. military presence in that country, but there is almost no debate on the question. And when liberal Illinois Sen. Richard Durbin argued that the White House should acknowledge that the United States is engaged in "hostilities" against the government of Libya and seek congressional approval under the War Powers Act, he hastened to assure his colleagues and Obama that he would oppose cutting off funds for the Libya war.

Liberal institutions; a few major journals of opinion; feminist, civil rights, and labor organizations; and intellectuals such as economists Paul Krugman, Joseph Stiglitz, and Robert Kuttner nip at the heels of social and foreign policy, for example urging the administration to address the crisis of 25 million jobless and underemployed Americans. But during the two-year-long presidential campaign that began in 2010, liberal commentators, with only a few exceptions, such as Chris Hedges and Robert Scheer, carefully avoided direct criticism of the Obama

administration's right-wing policies, including the relentless deportation of more than a million undocumented immigrants, the ruthless
killing of suspected terrorists—some of them American citizens enti-
tled to indictment and trial—and the continuation of the torture
program. Even as liberals direct their fire at the right, they capitulate to
it. They are in thrall to their hope that Obama and the Democrats really
do mean to change things, that the president's compromise-and-parry
fancy footwork is prologue, not final policy. Lurking beneath this hope
is fear: the twin specters of extreme right and left. Beyond Obama lies
the abyss. What is the basis of that great fear?

In the American political unconscious lurks a dark, but pervasive
drive. Since World War I, a very large portion of the population has
thrived on war and war preparation. Among other things, war relieves
unemployment, and the ghost of the Great Depression still haunts the
imagination of the unions. That the United States has long been in an
epoch of permanent war can easily be shown. It has the largest standing
army in the world and directly employs a million men and women who
would otherwise join the jobless in an already cluttered labor market at
home. As the police force for the industrially developed world, it spends
more on arms than all the nations of the European Union put together.
For most of the post–World War II period, its military contracts have
supported millions of jobs and brought in a substantial portion of the
profits of major corporations in the auto, steel, high-tech computer, and
automation industries. Hundreds of U.S. communities owe their
economic viability to military bases. The United States also maintains
more than 250 foreign military bases. No wonder, then, that the large
industrial unions and their leaders have been vocal supporters of military contracts and often ally with their employers to lobby Congress on
their behalf.

To sustain all these benefits requires that the country have a permanent enemy. From 1917 through 1991, Russia and then the Soviet bloc
supplied that requirement. George Kennan's famous 1947 memo
declared the policy of containment, portraying the Soviet Union as
expansionist, a declaration that seemed to be proved by its military
occupation of and eventual political hegemony over most Eastern
European states, and its acquisition of the atomic bomb in 1949, when

the United States lost its monopoly in nuclear weapons. The doctrine of Soviet expansionism and the addition of China to the potential enemies list—also in 1949—justified support for the growth of the American military. It also justified ideological anticommunism, which pervaded not only the center-right national administrations and the Congress, but also the liberals and their labor movement allies. In fact, the key figure of the labor movement's progressive wing, the United Auto Workers' Walter Reuther, not only became a fervent proponent of defense contracts as a major jobs program but also was a devout anticommunist within the liberal camp. The UAW he headed had no room for communists, nor did he evince more tolerance for anti-Stalinist radicals, most of whom were self-declared revolutionary socialists.

Some unions actively collaborated with the government's assault on the communists. For example, a number of seafaring and waterfront unions cooperated with the Coast Guard and the FBI by identifying activists who were alleged communists; others, such as the industrial unions, refused to defend members who were fired by corporations after being subjected to government or Congressional charges.[2]

McCarthyism, an Attack on the Unions

Since the 1936 presidential election, when a protofascist third party, the Liberty Party, emerged in the face of the Republican collapse before the dazzling success of the New Deal, liberals have attached themselves to the Democrats, sanctifying them as saviors of the people and a shield against the right. This feckless stance was reinforced during the grim McCarthy years, when suspect government employees were fired and the remainder forced to take a loyalty oath, communists were put on trial, and countless radicals were persecuted with jail terms. In the 1950s, most unions, the media, and liberal and agricultural organizations also purged their staffs of Reds, and Hollywood blacklisted many of its major talents.

With a handful of exceptions, the liberals fled from their own civil liberties principles and, perhaps more egregiously, from politics itself. Most were silent as democratic rights were trampled—they were glad to be rid of their "dangerous" radicals and terrified of opposing the authorities. Of course, as Ellen Schrecker has shown, the real target of the anticommunist hysteria and its central thrust was the labor movement. While roundly condemning McCarthy for his excesses, the leading left-liberal trade unionists, like Walter Reuther, conducted their own internal witch hunts and succeeded in ridding their unions of the communist left. Meanwhile, intellectuals rationalized their own collaboration with McCarthyism by arguing that the Communists were not a legitimate U.S. political party but rather agents of the Soviet Union, a conspiracy masquerading in the garb of democracy. Others quixotically celebrated what they perceived as the expansion of freedom for anticommunist intellectuals, and turned their eyes away from the spreading terror that prompted the government to deport radicals and some American-born radicals to voluntarily leave their own country, and others to go into hiding. The eminent liberal critic Lionel Trilling led the pack of so-called New York Intellectuals in "choosing the West" as the lesser evil in a polarized world. Some, like the philosopher Sidney Hook, and *Partisan Review* editor William Phillips, actively collaborated with the CIA in purging cultural organizations of both Communists and independent radicals who refused to view all Communists as agents of the Soviet Union.[3]

The overt state terrorism practiced by Democratic and Republican administrations alike from the late 1940s to the 1960s may seem a thing of the past, but political repression remains an underlying force in American politics. We dare not openly debate alternatives to a capitalism that embraces the permanent war economy. The word *socialism* is enough to send many supposed advocates of publicly financed health care into compromise or denial of their own cause. And although there are many radicals and Marxists "of the (comfortable academic) chair," few of them are prepared to voice their ideology in the popular forum. They teach and write scholarly works, but scared by memories of the Great Depression and the threats of an uncertain economic and political situation today, they will not risk living a public life that carries with it potential costs; they will not openly oppose the system per se.

In short, the prevailing quest among progressives, as among the general population, is the quest for security, for the certainty that tomorrow will be no worse than a repeat of today. There is little tolerance today for visionaries, for people willing to plunge into the unknown. In fact, as the epidemic of mental illness and prescription antidepressant drugs attests, tens of millions are seeking refuge from what they experience as mounting personal disasters. As the political intellectual C. Wright Mills often reminded us, in America, public issues are often experienced as private troubles. We want no movers and shakers to disturb our mental tranquility, even if that peace is bought across the counter, a temporary and artificial escape.

And many liberals are still afflicted by the memory of the 1960s New Left, which directed its fire not just at the right but also at them, for forsaking the fight for a just world. Former radicals who had drifted to the center, like Daniel Bell, Arthur Schlesinger Jr. and Seymour Martin Lipset, made it a special project to repudiate the left, calling its "minions" immature and irresponsible. They even engaged in red-baiting, when some student activists during antiwar protests declared their support for the Vietnamese Communists.

In fact, these apparent harbingers of mass radicalism—the New Left, parts of the student movement and the militant wing of the black freedom movement—were the last moment of their kind: the concrete enactment of an outburst of liberal rage. For the first time since the 1920s, a visible left surfaced and released a vast quantity of elemental—even libidinal—political energy. In addition to committing acts of resistance, both civil disobedience and occasional violence against objects of capitalist and military power, it advanced concepts such as participatory democracy; genuine sexual as well as economic equality; communal living; revolt against alienated labor; guaranteed income and even socialism. These ideas raced through the hearts and minds of young people—their conservative opponents might have said, like a contagious disease. In fact, even most of the liberal faculty at Harvard, Yale, Columbia, Michigan and elsewhere recoiled at the rebirth of student activism. They saw little reason for university reform, distanced themselves from the teach-ins against the Vietnam War, and turned their collective back on black students' demands for academic programs that addressed black history and culture. Liberals became some of the most forthright defenders of the universities even as those institutions moved toward corporatization and increasing reliance on the military for their sustenance. Liberal intellectuals insisted that universities were bastions of liberty and that the New Left was an authoritarian movement bent, perhaps unintentionally, on the destruction of liberty. Radical professors, meanwhile, did not feel the benefits of the university's supposedly free exchange of ideas. Columbia University's tiny coterie of radical professors were so effectively isolated, several left to take jobs elsewhere.

That classic liberal slogan of the French Revolution, Liberty, Equality, Fraternity, rang out once more in the 1960s and early 1970s, and most modern liberals were not pleased. Having discovered their fealty to the status quo and their fear of the taint of radical opposition, many embraced a new principle: compromise with the eighteenth-century branch of liberals—the conservatives.

We are currently witnessing the resulting variations on traditional liberal ideology. The time-honored watchword Equality has been replaced with Diversity. What R. H. Tawney, writing in 1920, called the acquisitive society may permit a plethora of identities, but it has nullified the aspiration for more equality. Former key liberal ideas such as redistributive justice—that is, significantly higher taxes on the rich to correct the inequalities of the market—and community control of key institutions such as schools have all but vanished from the modern liberal's creed. The notion that the state can level the class playing field has no high-profile supporters. And although liberals mutter about unemployment, the self-evident idea that shorter hours would produce more jobs than any program of government spending has been stricken from the conversation. Even the labor movement—the folks who brought us the weekend—has abandoned its most subversive demand: less alienated labor. In the recent struggles around the public-sector budget crisis, unions have granted the states substantial concessions in order to preserve jobs. Nowhere is a program for shifting the burden of the crisis from working people to Wall Street and the upper middle class being advanced as a serious alternative to draconian cuts in wages and benefits.

There has been a steady rightward drift among intellectuals since the 1960s. Tenure, a system originally instituted to prevent arbitrary firings, has become a reward for adequate scholarship and teaching. The erosion of its purpose over the decades has occurred in the context of endless fiscal crises for education and the state, producing an underclass of disenfranchised part-time teachers and untenured full-time faculty who remain politically silent and publicly inactive so as not to jeopardize their prospects for tenure in the future. Even liberal tenured faculty are politically circumspect, especially in the few hundred elite colleges and universities, where relatively ample salaries and amenities encourage complacency. The new union activism among part-time and some full-time faculty has risen mostly in chronically underfunded public institutions, where it carefully presents itself in the garb of conventional trade unionism. Few have been willing to step beyond the boundaries of acceptable action, at least before Wisconsin's public-sector teachers and professors and their student allies broke the mold. And their backs were to the wall.

We live in a time when liberal reform is dead. Not just because capital has waged a successful war on labor and the state's social-wage programs, but also because the liberal opposition is fragmented, their organizations shriveled, their leadership intimidated by attacks from the right and driven into a corner, where they huddle impotent. In this political moment, liberals are ready to offer an olive branch to their adversaries: "Cut back Medicare and Social Security, but modestly raise taxes on the wealthy as a symbolic gesture so that we can save face." They have permitted the right to seize the initiative; all, except for a few exceptional unions, are still plagued by the ghosts of radical movements stifled in the past, and the specters of McCarthyism and fascism send them scurrying into the arms of the neoliberals. In fact, the distinction between the social welfare liberals and the pro-business neoliberals has all but vanished. Despite encouraging signs of organized discontent, most of the left is still in the grip of that mass psychology of fear. The risk-takers have been relegated to the margins, vastly outnumbered by those who seek security, conformity, and compromise. The decline of the radical imagination hobbles attempts to resist the system, let alone to create alternatives.

Capital is destroying the lives of the majority whose work—or lack of work—supports it, yet it survives, thanks to the eclipse of the radical imagination, the absence of a viable political opposition with roots in the general population, and the conformity of liberal intellectuals, all of them subjugated to the great fear. Will there be life after this death?

Occupy Wall Street: Promise and Problems

The Occupy Wall Street movement was long in coming, and is certainly a sharp departure from the usual protest: instead of a one-day demonstration, a 24/7 encampment; instead of a list of demands, a stark indictment of wealth concentration. This movement seeks not justice within the prevailing system but rather a massive redistribution of wealth. Unlike the Madison Spring protesters, whose direct action gave way to electoralism, the Occupy protesters have disdained to be co-opted by any party and describe themselves as postpolitical. Within itself, the movement has revived the almost forgotten practice of "participatory democracy," last seen only in the leading edge of the New Left back in the 1960s. Let us recognize these achievements but focus, instead, on what comes next, given the movement's strengths and limitations.

After Occupy Wall Street's dramatic beginning, several events altered the movement's landscape fundamentally. A New York winter made outdoor encampment difficult. The tent city at Zucotti Park was a temporary solution, at best, yet the tents overwhelmed the scene. How could Occupy avoid becoming a social service organization when homeless people and other deprived souls joined the encampment? And despite the movement's spread to more than 100 cities and towns around the country and in Western Europe, and the huge Oakland march that shut down for a day the fifth-largest U.S. port, nagging questions remained. Could this purportedly leaderless uprising craft an organizational plan that would help it survive times of consolidation rather than forward motion? Were there other objectives beyond the sweeping call for income redistribution, a call that has been interpreted by liberal politicians as raising the taxes of the very rich? Although it was a stroke of genius for the assembled protesters to refuse to reduce their resistance to a set of manageable demands, how long could such a protest and resistance sustain them?

Yet Occupy's core statement was in fact a cogent one. By calling themselves "postpolitical" they chiefly meant that they refused to become entangled in mainstream electoral politics. But the movement offered a class analysis when it posited 99 percent of the population as have-nots and 1 percent as haves. (In fact, these figures were conservative: U.S. wealth is concentrated in the hands of only 0.01 percent of the population, one hundredth of one percent.) But posing the conflict in these terms masks certain aspects of the protest, and chiefly that this largely began as a movement of the dispossessed "new" middle class: salaried, credentialed professional workers, who unlike the old middle class are neither self-employed nor owners of small businesses. Of course, since the protest began, older people, unemployed and employed nonprofessional workers, labor unions, and progressives have joined the fray. Since the Depression of 2007, they have all discovered that the economy no longer has room for most of them. But their alienation is more than economic. Joblessness and declining material prospects may be solved within a political system willing to accommodate at least some of the disaffected. What the system cannot do is address the political and cultural disaffection that economic alienation has bred. Like the New Left, whose members for the most part shared the material comfort produced by the United States' favorable position in the global economy and its domestic advantages as a permanent-warfare state, the current generation of the "new middle class" harbors a deep critique of the system, one that cannot be healed by the same left-liberal program of jobs, jobs, jobs. Too many of the jobs produced now do not heal the lives of those who take them.

The rise of temporary work as a labor solution has cast a huge shadow over the professional and technical caste. People must take these jobs, because a paycheck is still the major source of food on the table and a roof over one's head. But very few jobs now offer real fulfillment, professional or material. For millions, life has become precarious. Increasingly, the job as an institution is under siege, because employers—public and private—hire only on a contingent or contract basis and do not offer health care coverage, pensions, or paid holidays and vacations to a substantial portion of their workforce. In short, the precariat has expanded to include the new middle class, and once privileged professionally and technically qualified workers have even joined the proletariat, working in service jobs when they cannot find work—even precarious work—in their own fields.

The political system has failed to address this dimension of the crisis economically and is even less capable of addressing the social and cultural alienation it has caused and that marks the Occupy revolt. College graduates are waiting tables in third-rate restaurants where tips are small and steady work is almost nonexistent. Low wages and temporary employment have forced young people to share apartments and other living costs. Those who want to live alone or with a partner are obliged to hold down more than one job. The traditional labor movement once boasted that it brought us the weekend; the decline of traditional unions and the burgeoning of the nonunion service economy has taken away Saturday and Sunday for many. Will the Occupy movement articulate the broader dimensions of labor alienation, beyond income disparity? Will it become the social movement of a generation? So far, there are few indications that it will lead a public discussion about these issues.

Finally, there is the question of organization—a perennial agony for movements of protest and resistance. The Occupiers have understandably distanced themselves from a variety of predatory political forces, ranging from Tea Party libertarians and left-liberal Democrats to the seriously weakened socialist and communist groups. They reject the conventional forms of hierarchy, both for their own movement and for society. Internally, horizontalism has become an inviolable mantra and practice. The movement's activists hesitate even to pose the question of whether to allow some formal organization—opening an office, implementing some type of practical governance—fearing that participants will see this as a return to hated bureaucracy. Even to hint at the question has become risky in a movement where spontaneity has been elevated to the status of a religion.

The Occupiers might do well to examine the history of radical organizations. They would discover previous efforts, and not only by anarchists, to implement democratic forms of order that resist the normal patterns of elected leaders and representative government, for example, governance by federation rather than by central bureaucracy. In this model, a movement is united by coequal participants who may send delegates to coordinating meetings. Another form is the workers' council, with popular assemblies that occasionally reach outside the workplace into the neighborhoods. Of course, there is a danger that any form of organization may evolve into a hierarchy. That is what destroyed

Students for a Democratic Society, the leading organization of the New Left. But the SDS was also plagued by ideological conflicts, and conflicts breed inequalities, organizational as well as social and political.

Federations and popular assemblies presuppose a general agreement among participants over principles and analysis of the situation the organization has been formed to deal with. In order to achieve these principles, a relatively long period of discussion and education is necessary. Two years after its appearance, the Occupy movement failed (or refused) to initiate these processes in a sustained way. In New York and elsewhere, under the rubric of the Free University, it sponsored some short educational symposia but had no longer-term strategy for putting ideas at the center of its activity. The Occupiers also refused to craft a permanent organizational structure that could sustain the movement during less active periods. When asked whether Occupy intended to address these practical and ideological questions, organizers admitted, privately, that to do so might split the activists they had.

Occupy lives on as a floating social service. It bravely intervened during Hurricane Sandy, providing food, water, and other supplies to isolated Rockaway and Staten Island, and to New York residents who had lost electricity and had little or no mobility. In this respect, it outperformed the much better financed American Red Cross and New York City government; the *New York Times* acknowledged Occupy's contribution to relief efforts, and for a moment the movement was back in the public eye. Some Occupy groups around the country have entered the fight to reverse home foreclosures, with some success. But by the end of 2012 the movement had, at least temporarily, lost its signature presence as a site of protest. Whether it can go beyond its function as a service organization in future and expand its role in resistance movements remains to be seen.

Of course, there is a long history of radical social movements taking on the burden of social services. During strikes, in addition to participating in demonstrations and sympathy walkouts, the labor movement has contributed food and money to strikers as an act of solidarity. In the 1960s, when a group of miners in Hazard, Kentucky, organized a wildcat strike against their corrupt union leaders and the mine owners, who denied them access to the memorial hospitals, the West Coast

Longshoremen, the Teamsters, and the Auto Workers' local unions contributed food and funds.[4] Pete Seeger and other artists held benefit concerts, and student volunteers came to Hazard to assist the workers. The Black Panthers conducted breakfast programs and various relief efforts in Los Angeles, Chicago, and other major cities.

But in both of these cases, the movement's service work was part of an educational and organizing action, rather than a substitute for one. Unfortunately, in recent years services have occupied center stage for many unions. The activities of the welfare administrator and the business agent who handles individual grievances are the heart of most unions' enterprise. Education has virtually disappeared from the agenda; some unions have even suspended their newspapers, which were once a main source of union-sponsored information and propaganda.

The following chapters will examine these problems and the successes and failures of recent and past social movements in the context of political organization, and the possibility of new forms of organization with the force, commitment, and spirit to overcome the great fear that has protected labor injustice in our society.

CHAPTER THREE

The Rise and Fall of the
Modern Labor Movement

The Great Depression drastically reduced union membership; in 1931 less than 10 percent of the labor force was organized. Union membership fell during the 1920s as rail, textile, and garment strikes were crushed. But from 1929 to 1932 unions were reduced to a small fragment of the labor force, except for the miners, apparel workers and a few crafts. But 1933 witnessed the beginning of a modest economic recovery and some unions grasped the opportunity to reverse the decline. The movement was reborn as miners, garment and men's clothing workers unions struck for higher pay and union recognition, and by 1940 more than 11 million workers had joined unions in a wide array of industries, notably steel, auto, rubber, electronics and packing. Ironically, the AFL was a major beneficiary of this upsurge as well: Teamsters, construction trades, machine tools, food processing, and sectors of the retail trades formed the basis of AFL gains, but they also won a share of packinghouse, electrical manufacturing, metal fabricating, and the telephone industries. Traditional craft unions like the AFL Electrical Workers organized Western Electric and other companies on an industrial basis. The union's New York affiliate, Local 3, formed an industrial division, competing with the CIO's Electrical and Radio Workers. In Saint Louis a Teamsters local had a substantial industrial union membership, alongside its retail and warehouse members.

By 1953, more than a third of private-sector workers were represented by unions, the highest union density in American history. And after National Health Insurance failed to pass in 1949, benefits such as health care, supplementary pensions, paid holidays, and vacations became the norm for many workers, regardless of whether they were in unions.[1] Major corporations like IBM and Kodak and textile giants such as Deering Millakan and JP Stevens kept the union out by offering employees wages and benefits comparable to union standards. The NLRA outlawed company unions, but paternalism lived on, not only in nonunion companies but also in corporations like General Motors, U.S. Steel and General Electric, which saw certain advantages to themselves in cooperating with the unions. Some of the less "enlightened" companies, like Ford, and smaller steel corporations, such as Weirton and National, had to be forced into accepting union organization by the wartime Roosevelt administration.

Why did GM, U.S. Steel, GE, and other large, oligopolistic corporations agree to unionization? Part of the answer, at least for GM and the four major rubber corporations, was the factory occupations in Flint, Detroit, Cleveland, and Akron: they preferred peaceful organization to such baptisms of fire. And there may have been another equally compelling reason. Collective bargaining is one way to make labor a predictable factor in production. Of course, unionization obliged these major industrial corporations to yield higher money wages and assume the burden of the social wage (benefits), especially when the New Deal funds that provided elements of the social wage through federal taxation had been exhausted. On the other hand, the contract provision that addressed shop floor grievances through negotiation and arbitration was less disruptive and costly than strikes, slowdowns, and sabotage. The unions traded their autonomy for job security and a private social welfare arrangement. Contracts increasingly banned strikes for the life of the agreement. Equally important, the union often became an ally of the company in matters of worker discipline.

This alliance was not primarily a legal matter: collective bargaining is, among other things, an explicit partnership between company and union officialdom. Ostensibly, both are committed to observe the letter of the bargaining agreement, and when either party violates it, the elaborate grievance procedure replaces direct action such as "quickie walkouts" and slowdowns, which are prohibited under the contract. The CIO's Electrical Workers was among very few major unions that refused to sign no-strike agreements for GE and Westinghouse contracts, yet there is no evidence that its leadership was committed to direct action in preference to negotiated settlements of outstanding shop floor issues.

Today, well over 90 percent of union contracts have a no-strike clause, and under penalty of law, the union is required to enforce it. When, on rare occasions, the union violates this provision, the company can—and usually does—procure a court order to end the strike and fine the union or otherwise discipline its officers with other penalties, including imprisonment.

When the newly formed industrial unions first engaged in collective bargaining, many agreed to suspend the strike weapon but insisted on limiting contracts to one year in order to maintain a relative freedom of action. The one-year contract allowed the union to take into account changed economic conditions in formulating its economic demands. It also constrained the companies, which had learned how to delay grievance settlements under typical four- or five-step procedures. In some cases, the contract permitted the union to call a grievance strike when unsettled issues accumulated.

But after World War II, the once insurgent labor movement became part of the establishment. Prominent industrial union leaders like the Steelworkers' Philip Murray and the Auto Workers' Walter Reuther loudly proclaimed the advent of an era of labor-management partnership. When the UAW signed a five-year no-strike agreement with the auto industry in 1950, the next few years witnessed an outbreak of wildcat strikes against onerous working conditions, especially speedup of the assembly lines, and a backlog of unaddressed grievances. Although under the influence of the Cold War the once insurgent UAW president, Walter Reuther, had become a fervent advocate of capital-labor collaboration, he and his leadership colleagues were forced to modify the contract to allow strikes under certain conditions, including discharges and unilateral company changes in working conditions, mainly speedup. And the five-year contract was dead, at least in the auto industry.

However, the modified restoration of the strike weapon did not establish a precedent. Because the steel industry never experienced an upsurge, steelworkers signed longer-term agreements, and by the end of the 1960s most union contracts were at least three years in duration. The strike was not abandoned, but direct action increasingly took a backseat to grievance procedures and arbitration. Eventually the moment of upsurge arrived in steel, too, but under the changed conditions of global competition, the union was unable to hold on to its newly won strength.[2]

From Militant Organizing to Concessionary Bargaining

After World War II, unions did not abandon organizing altogether, but except in industries like apparel, textiles, and metal fabrication that had suffered from the deindustrialization of the North and Midwest, basic and leading consumer goods unions concentrated on serving existing memberships. Although the CIO Textile Workers devoted a large share of its resources to unionizing the South, particularly Virginia, Georgia and the Carolinas, its efforts met with limited success. In the upper South it did make gains, chiefly in the synthetic fiber industry, but across the Deep South one could count the number of unionized plants on one's fingers. Employers there had lost no time mobilizing their management, local governments, and religious institutions to oppose union drives. Often in one-industry towns, sites favored by the corporations, the union had difficulty finding a place to meet, and whatever venue it did find was put under constant surveillance; implicitly threatened by discharge or worse, many workers were afraid to show up. Unions in such towns simply lacked the resources to effectively conduct organizing on a scale that offered some protection to the workers. The several efforts by the CIO and later the AFL-CIO to conduct coordinated organizing among a group of unions in a specific geographic area suffered from strategic drift and bureaucratic stifling of organizers' initiative; equally, if not more, important was the labor movement's ambivalent stance on questions of race.

This was particularly evident in the CIO's Operation Dixie, conducted between 1946 and 1950. The CIO and Textile Workers Union of America

(TWUA) leaders decided to concentrate on the textile industry, whose workers were almost all white, except for those holding the most menial jobs. Other affiliates, like the Packinghouse, Fur and Leather, Mine-Mill, Furniture, and Food and Tobacco unions, all of which were part of the CIO's left wing, decided to focus their activities on plants where blacks were in the majority.[3] Their two-pronged campaign in these workplaces emphasized both economic gains and dignity, that is, they openly linked the union to the struggle for racial equality. In most cases, this strategy led to significant victories, especially in the huge R. J. Reynolds plant in Winston-Salem, North Carolina, but also in Charleston, South Carolina, several nonferrous-metal plants in Bessemer, Alabama and Memphis, Tennessee, and among tobacco workers in Raleigh-Durham, North Carolina. By contrast, the TWUA and CIO leaders carefully avoided race issues, believing they would immediately isolate the union. Of course, this restraint did not deter the textile corporations from using those issues to fight unionization. In one nefarious ploy, they published a photograph of CIO secretary-treasurer James Carey dancing with a black woman; the image was widely circulated in the South and became an emblem of the fear, sowed by employers, that unionization was a prelude to miscegenation. The left-leaning unions did not denounce the drive to organize the textile workers—indeed, they never ceased to plea for movement unity—but felt that attempting to start it by confronting a bastion of white racism was unwise. In fact, as the left-led campaigns developed, eventually whites joined and in some instances worked closely with blacks.

One more factor worked against the Southern organizing drives: the tragic defeat and aftermath of the 1934 national textile strike.[4] Historical memory does not vanish in twelve years; there were still many in the mills and textile communities who felt betrayed by the labor movement. It is difficult to measure its influence, but certainly the experience of 1934 left more than a scar: it remained an open wound.

Meanwhile, the CIO was moving rapidly toward full-throated anti-communism, and its leaders remained indifferent to the left-wing organizing strategy. Indeed, in 1949 and 1950 the CIO expelled eleven affiliated unions, representing in total more than a million members. Many of these affiliates had been successful but were considered an orphaned remnant of Operation Dixie. Operation Dixie was a victim of the movement's own ideological split: the liberal CIO leaders simply undermined the unity that would have been a necessary component of Southern organizing. The AFL and CIO's ambivalence regarding the emerging black freedom movement and the left's relationship to it remained a serious impediment to labor's future in the South.

Long before the more discussed exodus of industrial production to China, India, and Mexico, labor's failure to organize the South accelerated the process of industrial migration. Although unions still had impressive density in many major industries throughout the 1950s, by the 1960s and early 1970s plant shutdowns in the North were a common occurrence. The "runaway" shops were no longer a phenomenon only of the textile and apparel industries. Auto, steel, electrical, and furniture plants relocated, too, and as the movement lacked the will to either contest the closures of unionized plants or to organize their replacements in the South, union power in the industrial production sectors swiftly deteriorated. Seeing the decline of union efforts in the South, in the 1980s foreign companies began to build plants in Southern states with right-to-work laws that prohibit the union shop, which requires workers to maintain union membership as a condition of employment. Although UAW agreements provided that transplanted shops owned by U.S. corporations were subject to unionization, the autoworkers were obliged to organize foreign-owned plants, such as the facility Nissan opened in Smyrna, Tennessee in 1983, which has resisted several union drives to date. In fact, the union has failed to organize a single one of the thirteen foreign-owned plants that have come here from Japan, Germany, and Korea. In effect, the United States has become the preferred location for auto-plant building, because the right-to-work states, chiefly in the South and along the Southern border, are eager to attract business. They offer corporations lower wages and a nonunion work environment and often provide building subsidies, deferred taxation, free water and other benefits as well.

This is the easy answer to why unions have done so poorly: of course foreign companies build their facilities in these communities that offer a "union-free" environment. They also build them in rural areas where jobs are scarce and workers are, at least for a time, happy to have a steady income, even though it is usually below union standards. But there are other reasons for which the unions themselves bear responsibility. In this era of concessionary bargaining, desperate to prevent plant closures in the North and Midwest, in a number of cases the UAW and other unions have agreed to two-tier wage systems, and to benefits programs that require workers to contribute greater sums to their health care and pension plan, and they have relaxed work rules on the assumption that companies need more authority over workers in order to keep their plants open in the North. And collective agreements are now of longer duration.

For example, in 2012, after striking for three and a half months against concessions demanded by their company 700 Joliet, Illinois Caterpillar workers—members of the machinists' union—voted to accept a contract with a six-year wage freeze that also froze benefits. In return, they received a one-time signing bonus that was not incorporated into their wage. Over the life of the agreement, this bonus will average about $8.50 a week. Yet unlike GM and Chrysler, which were on the brink of bankruptcy when they requested federal bailouts and union concessions, Caterpillar was rolling in profits—$4.9 billion in 2011. The company's assault against its workers was motivated, simply, by confidence that in the midst of economic depression it could bring workers to their knees. During negotiations and the walkout it threatened to fire its employees and hire an entirely new workforce. In the end, although the local union leaders recommended that the contract be rejected, the district union that had negotiated the agreement prevailed.[5]

Meanwhile, most industrial and transportation unions have been powerless to address the accelerating pace of technological change that has drastically reduced their numbers. For example, in the past forty years the production workforce of the U.S. auto industry's Big Three—GM, Ford, and Chrysler—has declined from some 700,000 employees to fewer than 150,000, while the nonunion sector continues to add workers. So the unions have less ability to attract new members to their ranks, especially when during organizing drives the company makes information about union concessions available to the workers—concessions that have narrowed the economic gap between the diminished unionized and growing nonunion sectors of the industry over the past three decades. Workers are justified in viewing the union contract as a document of ambiguous value. Typically, it still contains some job protections, and it offers workers with enough seniority a living wage. But in production industries, new, younger workers gain relatively less from being union members, and every succeeding contract reduces the advantages of the deal.

The conclusion one might draw from the dismal record of the last thirty years of union concessions is that collective bargaining, once an effective, although two-edged, weapon in labor's struggle, has reached a watershed. Today, collective bargaining in production, service, and public sectors is more a blunt instrument of management than a workers' sword. There are a number of reasons why this is so. Certainly, the paramount factor is the historic three-way bargain between the unions, the state and corporate capital, which, as we have seen, chained labor to a legal framework that inhibited its freedom of action. It is true that for at least a generation, millions gained from this arrangement. But the regular wage and benefits increases that were characteristic of the post-war period until the 1970s presupposed the continued dominance of the United States in the global economy and global politics. When Europe and Japan revived from wartime devastation and became exporting nations, and when in the 1990s China emerged—with the help of American capital—as a potentially major economic power, U.S. capitalists moved to reign in workers' living standards by sharply resisting money wage and social wage demands. And companies lost no time introducing labor-saving technologies into the workplace, while demanding expanded management prerogatives aimed at increasing productivity, presumably to reduce labor costs. Claims of economic necessity formed the ostensible reason for capital's offensive. But as labor's share of the social product was sharply reduced by technological innovations, a more important reason became clear: the subordination of workers and their unions. That is, capital saw in the new world economic order a chance to reduce workers' power to determine working conditions and, especially, to limit its control over the pace of production.

Softened by the program of labor-management cooperation, by subordination to U.S. foreign policy, by the U.S. political system, and by what the German sociologist and political theorist Robert Michels referred to as the iron law of oligarchy—exemplified in the growth of top-down union administration—the labor movement has dwindled to a set of corporate-oriented institutions that at best function as service organizations similar to private welfare agencies. Many are insurance companies, or act as agents for credit card companies. For example, I am a member of a large (1.4 million-member) national union, the American Federation of Teachers, that offers high-interest credit cards, average-price auto insurance, long-term care insurance, and low-priced periodical subscriptions. It also spends a portion of my dues to support Democratic congressional and local candidates with the excuse that we need "pro-labor" legislators. In 2012 it sent a huge chunk of voluntary member contributions to the reelection campaign of Barack Obama. In their fear of the insurgent right, labor's leadership is prepared to accept paltry political returns in exchange for the guaranteed protection of federal and some state governments. Having given up hope and ambition for significant gains, they have settled for a status quo that increasingly deteriorates but falls short of absolute catastrophe.

Most labor leaders refer to their constituents as either members of the middle class or else as working families. They have no notion that anyone who labors for wages or a salary and has little or no control on the job is part of the working class, with interests that are different from—in fact, antagonistic to—those of the bosses, public or private, and their political supplicants. C. Wright Mills defined the new middle class as salaried employees, who often have professional and technical credentials and who all enjoy a high level of job security. Yet in the past thirty years, few such workers have had any job security. In that period we have seen widespread layoffs of industrial and public sector workers alike. Much of the formerly secure professional and technical class and industrial workers endure precarious conditions. The working class by that definition is expanding even as organized labor concedes many of its former gains, including job security. This helps explain the familiar refrain sung by labor leaders as well as management that ours is a time of "one-sided" class struggle. That the unions, except under extreme circumstances, have not been willing to engage capital in combat is a symptom of both their despair and their complacency. Many unions have suffered severe contraction, and their relative strength continues to wane, but they still have automatic check-off of union dues, except in the right-to-work states, which usually ban this practice. For decades, many unions adjusted to right-to-work regimes because they were located in states with few union members. The heavy-industry states like Illinois, Pennsylvania, Indiana, and Michigan were presumably safe from right-to-work offensives, and the liberal states with large public-sector unions—New York, New Jersey, Wisconsin, California, Oregon, and Washington—seemed politically safe.

Then, in 2010, the world was turned upside down. The Democrats suffered a major shellacking, losing the House of Representatives to the Republicans. Perhaps even more damaging was the wholesale turnover in state houses and legislatures. The GOP held thirty of fifty governorships, and in many states, the GOP now controlled both legislative branches. These right-wing victories, combined with the decline of union power, emboldened Republican state administrations and legislatures to impose once inconceivable limits on workers' rights—not only right-to-work laws but also, as we have seen, Indiana's and Wisconsin's bans on collective bargaining for public workers. Ohio labor did turn back an antiunion law by vote referendum, but Michigan's GOP brazenly enacted a right-to-work law while avoiding the glare of public hearings or debate. These attacks were well-financed by the Koch brothers and other ultra-right capitalists; the unions simply lacked the forces to effectively counter the right's offensive.

What accounts for the reluctance of American labor to fight after more than thirty years of unrelenting employer attacks on wages, working conditions, and workers' living standards? First, although collective bargaining is no longer able to match wages to rising prices for consumer goods, many workers are intimidated by not-so-veiled corporate threats to close plants if workers make "unreasonable" demands. These threats predated the onset of the depression of 2007 and have accelerated ever since. In an era when good jobs are scarce, unemployment may no longer be a temporary setback, especially for workers over forty.

In consideration of the imperative of job "security," many unions now grant deep concessions to management. The Machinists-Caterpillar settlement in Joliet, Illinois is an extreme example, but wage freezes or reductions are becoming a norm in many collective-bargaining agreements. The two tier–wage bargain agreed to by the UAW may not yet be common, but given the strategic position of the union and the industry, which employs over a million workers, unless the movement regains its militancy the concession, which reverses labor's historic demand "equal pay for equal work," could set a pattern for other union agreements.

Many public-sector unions are dealing with managements who sit at the bargaining table and offer no salary increases for years after the expiration of the contract. These freezes are not confined to Republican-controlled states. The Democratic-controlled governments of New York and California, secure "blue" states, refused to budge from their no-increase positions, even as they refused to raise substantial taxes on the wealthy. California public employees do have the right to strike, but New York's Taylor Law bars public workers from withholding their labor in order to improve conditions, evidently allowable under the United States Constitution.

The labor movement has always advanced when workers were willing to risk their jobs to make gains—and even, on occasion, willing to risk their lives. Throughout the nineteenth and twentieth centuries, many who fought capital were virtually exiled from their homes and communities, especially in one-industry towns, where mining, textiles, steel, or electrical manufacturing was the only game to play in. Under these circumstances, job security was won by prolonged labor struggle; it was the legacy of countless heroes who were willing to sacrifice life and limb for the workers' cause. Like academic tenure—the job security program for professors, most of whom are not troublemakers—when not accompanied by struggle, job security has become a way to fold workers into the system, to reward their acquiescence to the austerities imposed on them by capital.

The mass psychology of working-class fear differs from that of liberal fear. As unions represent a declining proportion of the labor force, they see themselves as unable to resist encroachments by capital that overthrow American workers' once permanent assumption that their living standard will continue to rise. Saddled with debt—home mortgages, tuition payments for their children, car payments and other bills—and without strong union support, workers feel that the income loss they risk in challenging corporate capital is too steep a price to pay. When a minority of workers reject concessionary agreements or even when the majority occasionally rebel against them, as happened in a contract struggle with Chrysler, both company and union leadership waste no time warning the rebels that rejection of the "best offer" may mean plant closure. At Chrysler, thanks to this kind of pressure, the contract settlement was resubmitted with almost no changes and was ratified by a dispirited membership.

There is yet another reason for labor's slide: the deep reverence harbored by the overwhelming majority of top union leaders for authority, especially the authority of the law. This awe for the "rule of law" has displaced the primitive awe of the father. Beyond penalties that might be leveled against lawbreakers, union leaders are truly in thrall to the legal system. They are deeply respectful of the courts; their obedience to judges' injunctions ordering strikers back to work, and to legislative and court decisions to water down workers' rights, demonstrates they operate with the tendency to safeguard their organizations' resources and respectability rather than assert their power. The local and state labor leaderships enjoy hobnobbing with mayors, governors, and other elected officials, and the national leaders are never more joyous than when they are invited to have dinner at the White House. Of course, Bill Clinton, who during his eight-year presidency delivered almost nothing to workers and their unions, was a master of this kind of flattery; Obama was slow to learn, but after the midterm shellacking of his party in 2010, he quickly absorbed Clinton's lesson.

Once an outlaw social movement, the unions are now a vital appendage of capitalist power. They still thrive on their former reputation as "new men" of power, but they have settled for the actual status of loyal lieutenants of the core capitalist and political institutions and their top players. Their major job is to discipline a potentially and sometimes actively resistant membership and to ameliorate, but not resist, rollbacks in workers' past gains. When they are unable to stem an insurgent tide from below, their job, as in Wisconsin, is to endorse and then attempt to sidetrack direct action. It is not a taste for perfidy as such that motivates them. The top leadership of the unions has simply lost its taste for combat, if it ever had it. The perks of office are too lucrative, given the legal and institutional limits to union power, to abjure. The formation of a self-enclosed oligarchy is reinforced by a growing tendency for professionals to climb to the apex of union office: lawyers, professional union representatives with little or no shop or office floor experience, and relatives of former union officers. James P. Hoffa, son of the legendary Teamsters icon, is a lawyer, but he has risen largely on his father's reputation; the Teachers' president, Randi Weingarten, is also a lawyer; her classroom teaching experience was, to be generous, brief. The key leader of the massive American Federation of State, County and Municipal Employees (AFSCME) does not typically spring from the clerical, maintenance, and professional sectors that make up the overwhelming majority of that union's members. On the other hand, construction and industrial union leaders are elected, in the main, from the ranks; many, though not all, were once shop-floor workers. But the most rapidly growing labor unions are the so-called white-collar unions. They are not *of and by* the rank and file even if they claim to represent the members. After leaving office, these professionals rarely return to the ranks they never inhabited. The life of a union official prepares even former rank and filers for other elite occupations, not for the shop floor.[6]

During the years when radicals organized rank-and-file caucuses like Teamsters for a Democratic Union or similar caucuses among New York transit workers and Chicago and Los Angeles teachers in the public sector, workers were encouraged to resist management threats and stonewalling of their demands. In many of these cases union victories were achieved, though they proved to be short-lived. But beyond the caucus movements, what is lacking in the workers' movement generally is a political formation capable of educating, agitating, and organizing resistance to labor's decline and able to offer alternatives to current labor law and union practices.

CHAPTER FOUR

The Struggle for Union Reform: Rank-and-File Unionism

Introduction

To understand the roots of labor's regression we must make a short visit back in time. Already softened by the relatively brief postwar prosperity, and satisfied by the labor movement's growth, union leaders were no longer inclined to wage the jurisdictional wars that marked the huge organizing momentum of the 1930s and 1940s.[1] Organized labor was ready to settle down. In 1955, after years of negotiations, the AFL and its rival, the CIO, agreed to merge. By this time the AFL was substantially larger, with some 10 million members to the CIO's 4 million. The AFL's Building Trades Department, with about 3 million members in electrical, plumbing, iron crafts, painting, and labor held a virtual monopoly of organized workers in that industry. And although CIO affiliates were dominant among unionized industrial workers—virtually all of auto manufacture, rubber, basic steel, glass, packing, and heavy electrical equipment were unionized—AFL unions had made significant inroads into some goods-production industries as well. Among these were workers in aircraft, machine tool manufacture, food processing, chemicals, metal fabrication, paper and lumber production, oil refining, bedding and furniture, and textiles, and all of them competed with the CIO affiliates. Throughout the 1930s and 1940s the two federations were constantly at loggerheads. The CIO accused AFL unions of making backdoor deals with employers to thwart the CIO during organizing campaigns. The industrial unions brandished their militancy against the more conservative AFL, which was suspected of being soft and often racist as well as authoritarian. Until 1950, by which time the CIO's left wing had been expelled, the AFL kept up a constant red-baiting refrain against its rival. After that, "cleansed" of its left (and much of its edge), the CIO was ready to talk merger, not least because many of its key affiliates were beginning to resemble their less democratic AFL opponents.

AFL industrial workers were often attached to craft locals that controlled their destiny; they did not enjoy autonomy in collective bargaining, union affairs, or political action. AFL craft unions tended to consign industrial workers within their institutions to "B" status, a sign of inferior union citizenship. AFL president George Meany and his CIO counterpart, Walter Reuther, heralded the merger as a boon to union organizing. They quickly moved to authorize a constitutional provision, Article 20, that banned "raiding" of one union by another when an affiliate was recognized by the employer and by law as the collective bargaining agent for a given group of workers. Article 20 also restricted affiliates' ability to make inroads into another union's sanctioned jurisdiction, and it established an arbitration procedure for settling disputes.[2] Thus, workers who were dissatisfied with the quality of their union representation could, under the law, decertify the existing union and reorganize as an independent, but could not call on another AFL-CIO affiliate to represent them.

AFL-CIO leaders were pleased to end the labor wars, but the claim that internal peace was a necessary condition for union growth proved incorrect. The historical record shows that the period of intense interunion conflict was also one of the most rapid periods of union growth in American history.[3] Competition may have been irritating, but it stimulated energy in established unions. Apart from the extraordinary second coming of the labor movement in the 1960s and 1970s among public workers—itself marked by acrimonious interunion competition—union organizing in the private sector in the more than sixty years since the AFL-CIO merger has been relatively weak. To be sure, there have been notable victories among California farmworkers, for example, and the Teamsters' membership expanded rapidly, owing to its aggressive organizing program, especially after it was excluded from the AFL-CIO for corrupt practices and was therefore free to raid. Teamster organizers could brandish the record of Jimmy Hoffa, who had negotiated the fabled national over-the-road agreement with the trucking industry that equalized wages regardless of region and claimed to offer a more progressive wage-and-benefits package than their AFL-CIO competitors. (Of course, the Teamsters did not always deliver.)

But aside from these and some of the embattled industrial unions whose base moved south after the war—textiles, apparel, furniture, transportation (even though successes were scarce)—organized labor has mostly settled for what is termed the service model of unionism. Following this model, the labor movement no longer expresses working-class demands. Of course, at the legislative level unions have proposed reforms that benefit nonunion as well as unionized workers. But on an everyday level the labor movement has become increasingly businesslike and business-oriented, and on foreign policy its AFL-CIO affiliates and those of leading industrial unions have been virtual adjuncts of the U.S. State Department, especially on issues involving Europe and Latin America. U.S. unions once played a crucial role financing and advising pro-Western unions in Italy, France, and several Latin American countries where the left had made inroads among workers. Now, however, a union's primary focus is its own members, settling grievances by a professional staff or full-time shop-floor grievers and expanding its social-welfare benefits program. The postwar years have also seen intensified union electoral activity, largely devoted to electing Democrats. Union electoral strategy has been mostly defensive; since 1966 the national unions' legislative agenda has gone absolutely nowhere, even when Democrats have occupied the White House.

Union complacency breeds worker disengagement and, in some instances, rebellion. With the exception of contract ratification meetings, the regular monthly meetings of most industrial unions have been sparsely attended. Some locals of the UAW and the Steelworkers have retained a two-party system for union elections, but most of the others in the union movement were and are dominated by long-tenured officials who have tolerated no internal dissent or organized competition.

Rank-and-file–based competition for union office is mostly character-istic of former AFL affiliates, although in the 1960s it was fiercely waged in the painters' union and in some West Coast building trades locals. But the real start of rank-and-file rebellion at the national level was the leadership struggle in the million-member United Steelworkers.

The Birth of the Rank-and-File Movement

After the historic 1936–37 Flint General Motors sit-down strike, which set the stage for GM's swift recognition of the UAW, United States Steel Corporation officials decided that discretion was the better part of valor: their chief sat down with CIO president John L. Lewis and recognized the fledgling Steelworkers Organizing Committee (SWOC), under Lewis's protégé Phillip Murray, for the entire chain of the compa-ny's mills. SWOC had a much harder time with the rest of the industry. A cluster of "little steel" corporations, led by National Steel's Tom Girdler, refused to follow U.S. Steel to the table and fiercely fought the union for years. The signal event indicating the hard road faced by the steelworkers' union was the Chicago Memorial Day "massacre" of 1937, when company guards shot and killed several demonstrators. It wasn't until the exigencies of World War II softened their resolve that "little steel" became organized as Ford had been. In 1942 the United Steelworkers of America was formed under Murray's leadership. He and his secretary-treasurer, David J. McDonald, ruled it with an iron hand. Among the CIO affiliates the USW was perhaps one of a handful of top-down unions that tolerated no formal internal opposition. Even so, Murray cooperated with the CIO's "left" until persuaded by the Truman administration and the Catholic Church to abandon his centrist stance. As CIO president after Lewis's resignation, Murray led the organization squarely into the Cold War camp.

When Murray died in 1952, McDonald succeeded him as USW pres-ident and Reuther became president of the CIO. By then the USW culture was firmly in place. McDonald followed Murray's high-handed playbook to the letter. Before the decade ended, Joseph Malony, director of the union's Buffalo district in upstate New York, ran for USW vice-president against McDonald's candidate, Howard Hague. He lost, but the union remained in perpetual turmoil throughout the next twenty-five years. In 1965, the USW's secretary-treasurer, I.W. Abel, attempted to unseat McDonald and won by a narrow margin. But the real challenge to the Murray-era leadership came in 1977, when Ed Sadlowski, a Chicago steelworker and insurgent director of the union's largest district, 31, ran for president under the banner of a rank-and-file caucus against Lloyd McBride, Abel's chosen successor. A bitter campaign ensued, Sadlowski was defeated, and it was not long before the rank-and-file caucus was relegated to obscurity and finally dissolved.

During the 1980s and '90s, technological innovations—mounted in spite of a clause in the contract that limited management's right to introduce new technologies without union review and consent—combined with the revival of Europe's and Japan's steel industries to sharply reduce employment and limit output in U.S. steel mills. In 1959, a national strike called to preserve labor's rights regarding technological change lasted 116 days. There were then 600,000 workers in basic steel. By 2010, there were fewer than 100,000 working in the mills, although production of basic steel had not declined, except in proportion to total use. For the first time in more than a century of steel production, foreign-made steel exceeded domestic output in U.S. capital markets. The industry's management had made bad investment decisions that limited productivity and the union had not contested them. But the underlying problem went deeper: like the oil and chemical industries, steel experienced a computer revolution that eliminated many steps in the labor process.

The 1980s and 1990s were the decades of labor's retreat. Perhaps the most distressing symptom of the movement's decline was its downward slide in the auto, farm equipment and heavy truck industries, most of whose labor force were members of the United Auto Workers. During these years, the UAW's New Directions Caucus, led by Jerry Tucker, a former director of the union's St. Louis region, challenged the top leadership's concessionary approach toward industry management. The caucus made significant gains among autoworkers in the Midwest, the traditional heart of the industry. But by the 1980s, with UAW leadership support, the Big Three companies had already decentralized auto production, sending much of it to the South. In turn, the union had diversified, expanding its organizing to metal fabricating, public sector employees, and, in the 1990s, to graduate students in states where the union had considerable visibility. New Directions was unable to make headway against these developments and finally disappeared, although remnants of it retained a relatively strong influence in some Midwestern locals.

Rank-and-file discontent with established leadership reached its high point in the Teamsters union. In 1976 (the same year the Steelworkers were roiled in their conflict), several rank-and-file organizations, meeting at Kent State University, formed Teamsters for a Democratic Union (TDU). Its stated purpose was to transform the Teamsters from a top-down, employer-friendly, corrupt and often mob-controlled organization into a member-controlled democratic union. Its program included "direct election [of] officers; majority rule in contract votes; fair grievance procedure with innocent until proven guilty procedures; and no multiple salaries for union officials; an end to race and sex discrimination; and 25-and-out pensions." TDU was to be a membership organization with local chapters. From its founding convention until 1991, when the TDU's candidate for union president, Ron Carey, defeated two supplicants of the incumbent administration,[4] TDU had succeeded in winning many of the program's demands, notably the right of members to vote directly for top officers. The fifteen-year struggle to form a clean rank-and-file run union that was not corrupt seemed to have been successful. Carey, a Queens, New York local union president in the United Parcel Service (UPS), was not a TDU member himself, but he fiercely advocated for democratic, anticorrupt unionism. He campaigned barn by barn, a style that contrasted sharply with that of most top leaders, who generally rely on their political machines and conventional direct-mail advertisements.[5] Having elected its entire slate, TDU, with the help of its independent allies, made significant strides during Carey's first five-year term

Carey won reelection in 1996 against James P. Hoffa, a lawyer and son of the famed James R. (Jimmy) Hoffa, whose record of aggressive bargaining still resonated among many older Teamsters. The crowning achievement of the Carey administration was its organization of a two-week strike in 1997 against the United Parcel Service; the key demand was an increase in the number of full-time jobs in the company, whose policy was to hire thousands of part-timers. For a year, Carey employed his signature "barnstorming" strategy to help mobilize the membership for a possible strike. When UPS remained obdurate, refusing to create more full-time jobs or significantly close wage gaps between full- and part-time workers, the union was ready for a fight: 185,000 UPS workers walked out. They won the strike, gaining 10,000 new full-time jobs, a ban on subcontracting, and large pay and benefit increases.

But the added victory of consolidating the reform slate was short-lived. The same year, federal investigators found that outside consultants to the 1996 Carey campaign had illegally supplied $220,000 to his reelection bid, some of which had landed in the consultants' own pockets. Under fire, Carey stepped down, though he was later acquitted of charges of illegal activity. The election officer appointed under the federal Labor-Management Reporting and Disclosure Act ordered a new election; Hoffa defeated Carey's successor Tom Leedham and Hoffa's slate replaced much of the TDU/Carey-supported executive board.

Despite these tribulations, TDU survives to this day as the longest-lived rank-and-file organization in the unions. And although Hoffa remains in power and has defeated three TDU supported rank-and-file slates since 1998, after more than thirty-five years of its existence TDU is still a force in the Teamsters union. And it has remained a labor reformer: advocating for decent contracts, anticorruption policies, and reduced pay for top officers and many officers in larger locals and supporting shop-floor struggles for workers' rights. At the same time, it generally avoids ideological and electoral politics. TDU and the organization that remains at its center, Solidarity, is a movement in the syndicalist tradition, believing that any new society must be based on strong, democratic labor unions. Solidarity has spawned several other rank-and-file insurgencies, with mixed results.

Solidarity's most sustained, and dramatic, victory after the TDU elections of 1991 and '96 was the bid by the New Directions caucus of the 37,000-member Local 100 of the Transport Workers Union (TWU). Local 100 is the union of subway, bus, and maintenance workers in the New York City mass transit system. Formed in 1984, New Directions drew its core activists from members of Solidarity, many of them ex-students who had decided to realize their political beliefs not through professional careers but instead in blue-collar jobs. Like many leftists, they believed the key to fundamental social transformation was a militant and radicalized working class. They chose transit based on several factors: it had a large union with a colorful, militant history, that had struck or threatened to strike numerous times; it had a substantial black and Latino membership; and in most job classifications it paid a living wage, at least in comparison with many other industries that employed manual workers. Moreover, transit was a vital sinew in New York City's economy. The subways and buses carried millions to work every day. And, despite an anticommunist purge in the 1950s, the local had experienced a series of rank-and-file opposition movements since the 1960s, of which New Directions was the most effective.

The insurgents' fight had to be waged on two fronts: against management and within the union itself. The Metropolitan Transportation Authority, which manages mass transit in the New York area, was then among the most punitive of the area's public agencies, treating its employees with contempt and a level of industrial repression that resembled the nonunion era. Annually, the MTA filed 20,000 cases of disciplinary action against its 37,000-person workforce.

Since the 1960s black workers had waged an often heroic struggle, both for equality and against the MTA's oppressive policies. Ironically, under Roger Toussaint—the first black president in the union's history—the fight on the shop floor was largely forfeited. Over the years, New Directions had won elective leadership positions in several divisions, especially among the subway conductors and track workers, who were crucial elements. In sixteen years of opposition to a union leadership that they claimed was soft on management and had made successive contract concessions, New Directions ran three strong, although unsuccessful, campaigns under one of its major organizers, Tim Schermerhorn. Then, in 2000, they formed a coalition with other union dissidents to defeat two mainstream candidates, including the incumbent president. The coalition's 2000 standard bearer, Toussaint, not a New Directions stalwart, won 60 percent of the vote for president, and the opposition slate, also a coalition of New Directions and other dissidents, captured thirty-seven seats on the forty-six-member executive board. But not long after taking office, Toussaint proceeded to purge the union staff of its New Directions members and to ignore the mandates that he and the ND slate had received in the election.

The MTA also ignored the reform slate's program, which called for a change in management's draconian labor policies. Finally, in December 2005, violating the New York State Taylor Law prohibiting strikes by public employees, which had been enacted in response to the 1966 New York transit union's walkout, Toussaint led a three-day strike. The MTA immediately got a court-ordered back-to-work injunction, a $2.5 million fine against the union, revocation of the dues check-off, and a ten-day jail sentence for Toussaint (who served half of it). City and state politicians were nearly unanimous in their condemnation of the workers and their union. New York's Central Labor Council—the largest in the United States, representing more than 800,000 union members—ostensibly backed Local 100, and the city's labor leaders joined a mass demonstration to support the strike. However, the council did not call for other municipal and state employees to leave their jobs in sympathy, even for a day. Nor did they view Local 100's defiance of the law as an opportunity to invalidate the Taylor Law's no-strike provision. In the main, they were loyal to the existing law and respected their collectively bargained agreements, which prohibited strikes. But the reluctance of the city's union leadership to fight to rescind the Taylor Law has deeper roots.

When the court order came, Toussaint, who had to be goaded into the strike by five years of MTA intransigence, immediately called it off, leaving considerable bitterness among the union's membership. Later, he left Local 100 for a much less stressful position as the vice-president of the international union. The local's new president is, in some ways, a legatee of the rank-and-file movement, but the huge cost of the December 2005 strike still hangs over union affairs.

A Brief History of the New York No-Strike Deal

The drive by a number of national unions to organize public employees in New York began in earnest in the 1950s. Although the American Federation of State, County and Municipal Employees (AFSCME), two major teachers' unions, two Teamsters public employees' locals, and a few others lobbied city councils and state legislatures and conducted educational work among their constituents, until the late 1950s the chance of winning union recognition from city and state governments was virtually nonexistent. The big break came in 1961, when UFT, guided by American Federation of Teachers organizer David Selden, local AFT president Charles Cogen (a reluctant ally), and a small corps of working teachers (including a middle-school math teacher named Albert Shanker), threatened a strike and threw Mayor Robert F. Wagner into a panic. Although it would have been a minority strike—only 5,000 of the system's 45,000 full-time teachers were prepared to walk out—Wagner granted the union its demand: collective bargaining rights.

How did this happen? Selden, as Shanker later acknowledged, was a master of organization and tactics. A former Detroit teacher, Selden had been sent by the national union to New York City from Michigan in 1953 to organize the largest teaching city and administrative staff in the country. Once there, he found he had a hard row to hoe. The existing AFT local, he said, was little more than a debating society. The city government under the Democratic mayor was hostile to union organization among public employees. Even the legendarily progressive Fiorello LaGuardia, a strong advocate of unions, had opposed collective bargaining for workers in the public sector. New York's other unions, some of them among the largest and most powerful in the country, were mostly indifferent to public employees and particularly unsympathetic to teacher unionism: teachers were college-educated and their collective profile did not fit into a labor movement of more than a million industrial, construction, and transportation workers, many of whom were not even high school graduates. In general, the unions shared the prejudice that professionals—including teachers, doctors, nurses and many other categories of public employees—were not organizable.

Certainly, the CIO paid some attention to this neglected sector. It had chartered the United Public Workers (UPW), with which the left-wing New York City Teachers Union (NYCTU) was affiliated, and had a union of state, county and municipal workers, also under left-wing leadership. Neither organization was recognized by the city government, except for representing workers in grievance procedures. The

AFL had several white-collar affiliates, including the American Federation of Teachers, with which the New York City Teachers Guild was affiliated, and AFSCME. Neither the Teacher's Guild nor the small district council of municipal employees had bargaining rights. The United Public Workers were expelled during the CIO's anticommunist purge, and the AFL white-collar unions were largely ignored.

Selden changed that. By threatening a minority strike, he and his relatively small cadre among the city's public school teachers were able to persuade Wagner that it would be prudent to recognize them. Wagner was undoubtedly influenced in his decision by the health care workers' uprising that began in 1959 and that through direct action—strikes and demonstrations—had already organized thousands of mostly black and Latino low-wage hospital workers.

At the same time, an AFSCME organizer, Jerry Wurf, was sent to New York to organize blue- and white-collar municipal workers. Wurf's first efforts were directed at the parks department workers, most of whom had much in common with other blue-collar workers. District Council 37 grew slowly, but its efforts were bolstered by Selden's bold teachers' initiative and by the entrance of a competitor, Teamsters Local 237, under the direction of Henry Feinstein, a former CIO Public Workers organizer. Feinstein brought the remnant of that union into the recently expelled Teamsters. After several years of furious inter-union competition, DC 37 won the majority of a series of representation elections,[6] emerging with more than 150,000 members. Local 237 won in the Housing Authority and a number of skilled trades, mostly construction and maintenance in city-owned buildings, including the Housing Authority's, gaining a total membership of roughly 20,000. By the late 1960s most classifications of municipal employees were unionized: teachers, school secretaries and blue- and white-collar city workers, including several locals of professionals such as engineers, low-level administrative workers, and computer programmers.

The swift unionization of public workers in the 1960s that began in New York spread throughout the country like wildfire. It was a time of independent and sometimes radical social movements: the fight for black freedom and civil rights; the Vietnam War protests; women's liberation. These grassroots struggles electrified the country and its politics. The unions were fully aware of them and lost no time identifying themselves with the civil rights and—with the exception of the teachers' unions—antiwar and feminist movements as well. They had also learned from the AFT's effective political mobilization in New York City that the shop floor was only one front in the battle for union recognition. Public employees are state-builders, and they reached out to elected officials and political parties for support. Traditional private sector organizing regarded the state as part of the employer's antiunion arsenal, but during and after the New Deal the public-sector unions jumped with both feet into the political field.

When public workers organized, the price of union recognition was steep. Twenty years before passage of the Taylor Law, New York State's 1947 Condon-Wadlin Act prohibited public employees from striking. The Taylor Law increased the penalties for striking but sugarcoated the pill. The agreements that led to union recognition presupposed that the unions would not contest the antistrike provisions of the Taylor Law, because the law had been crafted to permit public authorities to recognize unions for the purpose of collectively bargaining over wages, benefits and working conditions. Union leaders hesitated to challenge the no-strike provision because of the perceived benefits accruing to recognition. It was not a deal made in heaven, for it deprived workers of a fundamental right, but after more than a decade of acrimonious competition and uncertainty, the union leadership was in no mood to start another fight. TWU Local 100 was crippled by organized labor's respect for and tacit approval of the Taylor Law. Even when the state labor council proposed some revisions of the law, in the 2000s, it did not seek to rescind the no-strike clause.

In 1974, Al Shanker, president of the large New York local, was elected president of the AFT, defeating his mentor David Selden, who had held the position since 1968. One of Shanker's major actions as local president had been to call teachers out on strike in 1968 to oppose three community-controlled school boards, in Harlem, Bedford Stuyvesant, and the Lower East Side, that had attempted to exercise jurisdiction over the assignment of teachers. Shanker and his colleagues preferred to deal with the central Board of Education rather than with the black and Latino leaders of these newly created local boards. The union succeeded in crippling community control over education for the next forty-five years.

Shanker died in office in 1997, after twenty-three years as AFT president. During his long tenure, the union had grown to almost a million members, but its chief competitor, the independent National Education Association (NEA) had more than twice as many. Still, AFT had won bargaining rights for teachers in America's largest cities—New York, Los Angeles, and Chicago—and prevailed in many medium-sized cities as well, including Newark, New Jersey, and Washington, D.C. Shanker's leadership was highly centralized, a style that rankled members of the largest locals—they called it Shankerism—but was nevertheless followed by his successors, Sandra Feldman and Randi Weingarten.

Beginning as a reputed militant, Shanker developed into a labor "statesman" who softened his approach to confrontation with school authorities, tightly aligned the AFT with the Democratic Party at the national and local levels, and counseled greater union "responsibility" toward school systems. The early Shanker had been inspired, following Selden, by the militant history of the Auto Workers and insisted that teachers should put aside their professional pretenses and act more like industrial workers. He later turned toward professionalism because he came to believe that teachers were unfairly treated by school authorities and the public and would no longer gain from militant action. He then urged the union to adopt a professional ideology as the best guarantee of job security. This standpoint entailed union sponsorship of more teacher credentials, professional development programs in the schools, and the introduction of pay rewards for teachers holding advanced degrees. Pubic relations gradually replaced the strike weapon and shop-floor militancy.

While municipal unions expanded, the cities faced a series of financial crunches. In 1975–76, New York City declared a fiscal crisis when the large financial institutions refused to extend their usual short-term loans to the city government unless the political establishment and the public unions agreed to severe budget reductions. The unions and the Democratic mayor, Abraham Beame, prepared for the worst, and they were not surprised when the city's finances were taken over by a bank-controlled Emergency Financial Control Board (EFCB). District Council 37 agreed to the layoff of 50,000 non–civil service employees, many of whom were black and Latino, and other municipal unions accepted reductions as well. Education budgets were slashed; improvements in teachers' working conditions were put on hold and pay increases were frozen and then reduced.

The United Federation of Teachers (UFT) accepted the financial board that Wall Street had forced on the city and also accepted the EFCB's proposal to transfer some of the municipal government's autonomous functions to the state. The union further endorsed the board's layoff of thousands of paraprofessional school workers, many of whom assisted classroom teachers. City government imposed unpaid furloughs on those remaining on the payrolls. Local union leaders, most of them Shanker and Feldman loyalists, all but abandoned their earlier industrial-union militancy.

Insurgency Among the Teachers

In the 1980s and 1990s, several rank-and-file caucuses emerged to challenge the UFT leadership in New York. These efforts were largely unsuccessful with elementary school teachers, but one of them, organized by the left, gained elective office among high school teachers, defeating a long-time Shanker-Feldman adherent, George Altomare. Although the UFT leadership regained power in high schools in the 2000s, many teachers remained restive. The office of billionaire mayor Michael Bloomberg gained firm control of the schools by dissolving district-elected school boards and centralizing the districts; it then began shutting "failing" schools, most of which were in black and Latino neighborhoods. School authorities were empowered to assign redundant teachers and those they deemed seriously flawed to a kind of limbo called the rubber room, where they continued to receive their salaries pending hearings but were given nothing to do.

The mayor's program corresponded to the Bush administration's No Child Left Behind, which evaluated teachers chiefly on the basis of their students' performance on high-stakes standardized tests. The union dissented from the policy, but only mildly. By the time of Obama's ascent to the presidency, this criterion for rating teachers had become dominant educational policy throughout the country. The two principal unions expressed some reservations, but carefully refrained from taking direct action to reverse national policy at a time when they had become fervent allies of Obama's.

In Los Angeles and Chicago, the 2000s were marked by opposition caucus victories. The Los Angeles teachers were the first to replace their Shankerite leaders. But it was the Chicago teachers' rank and file that really promised to bring a new day to the schools. Unlike the traditional unions, it moved beyond salary and benefit increases to demand a voice in the conduct of the system's educational affairs. Barack Obama's chief of staff, Rahm Emanuel, returned to Chicago and ran for mayor in 2010. The same year, Chicago Teachers Union presidential candidate Karen Lewis and a slate of members from the Caucus of Rank-and-File Educators (CORE) upset the long-entrenched CTU leadership, which in the eyes of the members was incapable of stopping the newly elected Emanuel from restructuring the system. Following passage of a 2010 law and using New York's mayor-controlled school system as a model, Emanuel's program promised to evaluate teachers, at least in part, based on student performance on standardized tests.[7] Emanuel further sought to extend the school day, on the premise that in order to learn better students needed more teacher time.

With Rahm in charge at city hall and Lewis helming the CTU, the die was cast for a major confrontation. In 2012, after many months of fruitless negotiations, the Chicago Teachers Union struck the school system for the first time in twenty-five years. The union sought a 30 percent salary increase to cover the increased teacher workloads and a hiring policy that guaranteed preference for laid-off teachers. It wanted an evaluation program that did not rely at all on student academic performance. And it demanded a voice in curriculum and professional development.

After two weeks on the picket lines, the strikers got a settlement. Under the terms of a three-year agreement, union teachers would receive three salary increases of 3 percent each—and a fourth if the contract extended to four years. The total raise could amount to as much as 17 percent for some union members, because increments were awarded to teachers with master's degrees. Further, "In case of school closings tenured teachers who are rated proficient or better are guaranteed first hiring priority in schools taking in students because of closings, if there are vacancies."[8] Under pressure from an impending court injunction, the union for its part agreed to the addition of ten more school days, though at the time of settlement the specifics were unstated. The CTU also gave up strict seniority rules in layoffs and rehiring. Its demands for a say in curricula were shelved.

In return for these concessions, the union's chief win, the salary settlement, might seem unremarkable—no better than the actual inflation rate. But compared to public employees' contract agreements elsewhere, it was a real gain. In New York City, for example, where all public sector contracts had expired in the previous two years, the city and state governments offered no salary increases to any union. This includes the United Federation of Teachers (UFT), District Council 37, and the Professional Staff Congress (PSC), an AFT affiliate and the union of faculty and staff for the City University of New York. Even so, the Chicago settlement did not satisfy many teachers there. In the winter of 2013, an opposition caucus announced it would field a full slate to replace the Lewis administration.

The Professional Staff Congress represents some 23,000 New York City workers: approximately 6,500 full-time professors and instructors; 12,500 part-time adjunct faculty; and more than 2,000 administrative and technical staff. In October 2010, the PSC's contract was up for renewal. Under New York state law, a previous contract's provisions remain in force until a new contract has been signed. The bargaining committee sits at the table negotiating some improvements, but for years the PSC had been absolutely stonewalled on salary increases. Other New York municipal and state unions had experienced the same treatment. At the state level, the huge Civil Service Employees Association (CSEA) signed a six-year agreement, the first four years with 0 percent increases and last two with increases of 2 percent. Probably if the municipal unions had agreed to this deal, they would have had a new contract. But, given the bargaining record of the 1990s, when they'd swallowed below-inflation raises, the prospect of four zeros was more than New York City unions could stand. Even unions like DC 37, which the government had traditionally used to set the pattern, were apparently unwilling to go along with the state's settlement.

The PSC, meanwhile, was prepared to fight, led by a rank-and-file insurgency called the New Caucus, formed in 1995 to oppose the complacent twenty-five-year local leadership that in the 1980s and 1990s had negotiated a series of concessionary contracts. The New Caucus campaign was waged on every one of CUNY's twenty-four campuses, and on some of them department by department. In its first contested election, in 1997, it won only a third of the vote, electing not a single member to the executive council. Caucus activists did not view the election as an unmitigated defeat, however, but as an organization-building action. The New Caucus had already won leadership at the chapter level on several campuses. During the next round of elections its candidates swept half of the chapters, though it continued to lose among staff. And by 2000, it was ready to win union-wide. It had raised $80,000 by holding a series of fund-raising events among its activists and sympathetic members and was able to hire a full-time campaign coordinator, produce professional-looking literature, send direct mailings, and conduct rallies at almost all of the campuses and units. It also ran an organizers' school. The curriculum included labor history, the history of public employees' and teachers' unionism, and strategies for organizing. More than seventy-five activists attended the six sessions, which helped raise the intellectual level of the second union-wide campaign, build solidarity, and raise morale. The New Caucus's progressive slate took office and prepared to take on the city.

The first three negotiating rounds yielded significant gains. Although constrained in their actions by the Taylor Law, the new leadership did not hesitate to stage demonstrations at meetings of the university's Board of Trustees, on campuses and in the central CUNY offices. Adjuncts won a paid office hour, full-timers' sabbaticals were more generously funded, salaries were lifted for all, with adjunct pay raised in somewhat higher proportion, just as some woefully underpaid technical and professional categories won substantially higher raises than those already better funded. In time, the PSC's old guard disappeared, and although a new old guard attempted to replace it in the 2009 election, they were unsuccessful. In the 2012 local union election, for the first time since taking office, the New Caucus ran unopposed.

Sadly, though the New Caucus has been able to maintain its position in the PSC, it has not been as able to build on its early successes at the bargaining table. After 2010, New York's city and state governments began taking a hard line, and neither the PSC nor the other unions have mustered the political will to educate and mobilize the rank-and-file for a risky strike or even mass direct action in order to break that stone wall. Arguably, the main burden of such a decision should be on the larger, more powerful UFT and DC 37. However, the leaders of these unions have been noticeably unwilling to risk their secure positions by engaging in illegal actions that would certainly entail severe penalties. If they feel their bargaining position is strangled by the Taylor Law, the smaller PSC leadership must be suffocating as well and may not feel strong enough to go it alone.

I was elected to the PSC executive council in 2000 as part of the New Caucus slate and was reelected twice. I attribute our victory to heightened membership awareness of what an aggressive union can do. As the New Caucus grew, we signed up thousands of adjuncts as union members and looked forward to our first chance to make good on our promises. I sat on the negotiating committee for three contracts. During my nine years in the leadership, the union made some important gains, built an alliance with members of the university's faculty senate and campus-based senates, extended our support to student efforts to limit tuition increases, and became a reliable ally of labor struggles both at home and abroad.

But certain aspects of the practices of collective bargaining, including the routines of grievance handling and the political commitments of our parent union, severely limited what we were able to do. We were also clearly hemmed in by the Taylor Law. Although eventually a portion of our leadership was willing to commit acts of civil disobedience outside the workplace, we were held, and held ourselves, to the restrictions imposed by the law. At CUNY, bargaining became a duel of wits that the university administration was willing to play, but as we learned, any settlement we reached with them required the evaluation and approval of the municipal government's Office of Labor Relations.

The OLR's criterion for approval was whether our agreement corresponded to its cost guidelines. Its method of cost evaluation clearly contradicted some of our own calculations, so we'd have to go back to the bargaining table for revisions. Since none of the city unions, including our own, was prepared to challenge the underlying premise of bargaining, the government always had the whip hand.

Collective bargaining became a game—How can we elude the rules without being slapped down?—or, worse, a ritual without substance. When raises were clearly on the agenda, if a union bargaining team had no ideas, it accepted across-the-board increases and did not fiddle with contract language, work rules, or established job classifications. New York's labor relations office knew which unions were bereft of imagination and started the round by approaching them first. The weakest, least creative union bargainers helped the city establish a pattern to which the rest of the public employees' organizations were expected to conform.

In general, this strategy has worked. Collective bargaining is effectually dead in most of the public sector, even if in most Northeastern states there are no political moves toward its legal prohibition, as there are in Wisconsin, or so-called right-to-work legislation, like that passed by Michigan's lame-duck Republican legislature and signed by its GOP governor. But the movements for union reform have reached a crossroads. To be sure, many unions can benefit from clean and effective governance and more rank-and-file participation in union affairs. But the era when union reform was enough to assure better contracts is, at least for the foreseeable future, mostly over. The union contract offers some assurances of wage and benefit levels, but work rules in almost all cases, even in the construction trades, are now determined by the employer. In industrial production, when workers refuse onerous, unilateral rules, the employer is likely to threaten plant shutdown, and there are plenty of takers in other states in a depressed economy.

It is important to take note of an alarming development at CUNY. Spurred by the national priorities of the federal Department of Education and a steady drumbeat sounded by business interests, the university's administration has recently invoked a general education policy that concentrates on science and mathematics to the detriment of the humanities. The avowed purpose of this policy is to improve students' job readiness, but its effect is to change the fundamental mission of the university. Moreover, CUNY has launched a major push in online teaching and learning, undoubtedly motivated, in part, by the budget crisis but also by a profoundly mistaken conception of pedagogy, culture, and what constitutes a real education. And in an educational culture so misconceived, are classroom teachers necessary?

And that touches one of the deepest reasons for the current malaise in labor: many workers are afflicted with security anxiety. Even before the 2007 depression, cuts in federal, state, and local budgets, along with a perception that the unions had little will to fight, tempered the workers' own willingness to risk their jobs. Just as in the production and transportation fields, in higher education the move to concentrate power at the top seems dominant, at least for the moment. Apparently, syndicalism has reached its limit.

Almost invariably, the spheres where industrial workers have retained a measure of control over the terms and conditions of their labor have not been mass-production shops but industries that make specialized products in workplaces not easily moved. Resistance has been somewhat more effective in transportation, especially on some East Coast waterfronts. However, the Teamsters union has been weakened by relentless employer demands that have transformed truck drivers from wage workers into subcontractors. After hundreds of companies went out of business or merged with the large carriers, many carriers began requiring drivers to buy their own equipment and paid them per load. Drivers no longer enjoy paid health care and pensions but must supply them from their contract income. Those who are still wage workers have experienced the fear that afflicts industrial workers who have suffered from plant shutdowns and technological displacement. Make trouble and the company might abolish union agreements altogether. Labor on a broad front is on the defensive and the reform movement has been defanged, at least for the present.

The issue now is not whether union reform is necessary, but whether it is sufficient to reverse the general slide of the labor movement. Where the numerous local reform movements have gained office, they do make a difference: grievances are more quickly settled or actively pursued; union affairs are more widely discussed and shared by members; progressive unions are more likely to commit acts of solidarity. Yet the reformers are still in the thrall of contract unionism, on the one hand, and on the other, their efforts are mostly directed toward their own members rather than to the broader working class in their communities, the nation, and the world. Finally, union reform addresses itself, generally, to full-time workers and largely ignores the changing nature of the labor market, especially the growing "precariat" of contingent, part-time, and temporary workers. With some exceptions, notably organized labor's support of the million people who participated in the 2006 national immigrant strike and marches, and its backing of the immigrant-initiated Florida tomato boycott, union reform movements, although important, are ultimately parochial interventions in American labor's decline.[9] In Chapter 5, I will discuss some of the developments in the changing labor force that pose significant challenges for a new labor movement.

CHAPTER FIVE

The Underlying Failure of Organized Labor

Technology and the Changing Face of Production

We are surrounded by technology. Everyday life is inundated with electronic media. Walk the streets, ride public transportation, attend a concert or any social event and one can witness a very high proportion of attendees, riders, and walkers texting their friends on iPhones, talking on cell phones, or listening to music on iPods. Critics ascribe this feature of contemporary life to the privatization of that life or, in a more comprehensive judgment, they conclude that technology has overcome the specifically human; accordingly, we *are* our technologies or, in a more modest view, have become part human and part machine. That is, in Donna Haraway's neat phrase, we are cyborgs. Haraway preserves the human element, but others, notably those who draw consequences from Martin Heidegger's essays on technology, are no longer certain that there is a human "species being" capable of resisting either the incursions of technology into everyday life or the biological shift signaled by our merging with the machine.

Political activists who are immersed in the use of social media ignore these philosophical ruminations and are barely aware of the impact of cybernetically driven technologies on the nature and quantity of work and of good jobs. They argue that the technological revolution has immeasurably benefited organizing and protest. The rapid spread of the Occupy Wall Street movement, they say, would not have been possible without the Internet, especially the transmission of images and texting on iPhones that provided instant communication. Many others who celebrate social media are impervious to critical discourses regarding the role these technologies play in the privatization and fragmentation of life, that is, in the gradual disappearance of the social. That they do reject or ignore this perspective seems irrefutable, given the nature of social-movement organizing. But it may be that today's social activists are victims of the obsession with the short term that afflicts us all. Almost exclusive focus of critics and practitioners on social media ignores the relation of technology to labor and the economy. In fact, the concept of the advanced industrial society and that of its complement the developing society are crucially linked to the degree to which each has applied the most efficient technologies to its agricultural, industrial, and services workplaces.

Obviously, all cultures engage with technology to some degree. From the invention of the spear and the discovery of fire, the harnessing of nature in the service of art—the original meaning of *techne*—has been built into human history. But the privileging of modern technologies has brought us face to face with "advanced" notions such as cost and efficiency. In a technical context, *efficient* means "labor-saving" or, more benignly, "productive". A society's degree of technological "progress" ultimately depends on whether the society has a scientific establishment capable of applying, if not generating, the theoretical underpinnings of the newest, most efficient techniques. If it does not, the high costs of technology transfer, entailing imports and dependency, tends to slow economic development, unless the country becomes a target of multinational corporations interested in industrial production. Even then, the developing country—Bangladesh, for example—may simply become a repository of low-tech production, such as apparel manufacturing.

China, by contrast, has invested considerably in the expansion of universities, technical schools, and freestanding research institutes, and now has a sophisticated scientific establishment, especially in physics. All of this has facilitated its emergence as a world economic power able to enter the small circle of developed societies. Yet because it initially chose to concentrate its industrial production on exports, at the expense of generating a strong internal market beyond the managerial and professional middle class—which would entail paying much higher mass wages—China is still dependent for its growth on the state of the global economy. When European and U.S. economies are mired in depression, Chinese industries slow down as well, and Chinese workers are laid off. If China's dramatic development of a mass rail system and its workers' revolts against nineteenth-century-style exploitation eventually yield living standards that invite the growth of an internal rather than export-dependent economy, the country will still face the great problem associated with technological innovation: mass unemployment. And that eventuality could help destabilize the current political system. These questions, already in full force in Western capitalist societies, demand a serious debate about the relationship of technology to work and to the character of social life.

We are perpetually treated to media assaults that remind us that progress, and indeed the fulfillment of the American dream for the vast majority of the population, is literally a function of the relentless application of technologies to the workplace, to health care, to education, to personal relationships. Physicians are increasingly tied to machinery; diagnosis has lost its qualitative dimension and is now largely dependent upon the numbers registered on scans, MRIs, and other tools. Educational achievement is largely measured by the numerical results students achieve on standardized tests; the content of learning is entirely subordinated, which signifies that the main measure of intelligence has become whether the student can strategically prepare for the examination, or even whether her parents can afford to send her to private preparatory programs such as Kaplan, Princeton, or their local equivalents.

Industrial production, both in capital goods as well as consumer goods sectors, is straining toward the automatic factory, a capitalist dream of the workerless workplace. If the U.S. steel, auto, and machine tool industries have survived the challenges of European and Japanese competition, that has been due in large measure to the application of computer-driven technologies to the labor process. That the consequences have been dire for millions of laid-off skilled and semiskilled industrial workers, who have suffered steep cuts in their living standards, is conveniently suppressed.

The propagandists who disseminate the unblemished benefits of the technological revolution—including a considerable portion of liberal economists and commentators—claim that in the long run Americans will benefit from the demise of the old Rust Bowl industries, even if in the short term some will suffer. Both liberals and the right vehemently deny that the final tendency of the contemporary technological revolution is to permanently decrease the number of good jobs. They also reject the idea that if jobs are to become scarcer, shorter hours and guaranteed income become imperative solutions, and that refusing them will mean an inevitable reduction in living standards for perhaps a majority of the population. Instead, they stress the importance of further schooling and job training to facilitate the workers' transformation from industrial laborers to what the former Secretary of Labor Robert Reich once termed "symbolic analysts." What is missing from this optimistic forecast is the ratio of workers made redundant by the new technologies to the number of new good jobs that the technologies create.

The other side of technological change is the race to the bottom. Over the past thirty years, the gradual disappearance of the mass industrial worker and the weakening of the unions based on the semiskilled workers and the degradation of skilled occupations to semiskilled status has resulted in wage stagnation and decline, large-scale housing foreclosures, and growth in the number of the poor, a class largely composed of former industrial workers—now unemployed, or low-wage, or condemned to part-time service work. And the "new poor," a class composed of the young, older workers, and some types of professionals, such as lawyers and managers, has not been created only by the depression that began in 2007; it, too, is partly the result of technological progress.[1]

Some glib boosters do acknowledge the social and economic costs of technological change. For most of them, the solution is to accelerate the expansion of schooling, both for the young and for displaced adults. Characteristically, and in conformity with the austerity thinking that has gripped much of America, the most recent proposal and practice is to fulfill the promise of new career education by offering online courses. Once the province of for-profit colleges, Internet-driven online learning has been dramatically introduced into the mainstream and is now sponsored by elite universities like Harvard and Stanford, some of the leading public research institutions such as Illinois, and the largest urban university in the United States, the City University of New York. Faculty at these institutions are encouraged to upgrade their Internet skills to be able to take advantage of electronic study aids such as Blackboard or, more extensively, to enlist themselves as instructors in online courses.

Online schooling is efficient because the electronic classroom can reach hundreds, thousands, or even hundreds of thousands of students while saving on the price of qualified full-time professors. Of course, unless an army of sub-instructors is available to lead discussion sections, the degree of interaction between teacher and student is extremely limited; indeed, some senior professors in the largest online sections prohibit students from contacting them individually. Given the austerity regime that continues to plague the public universities and the less-well-endowed private colleges, it is likely that the online instructor will simply supervise graders, who might be recruited from a pool of senior undergraduates.

This scenario does not, of course, preclude education in the conventional classroom. But if current trends accelerate, only a few hundred privileged postsecondary institutions will offer conventional classroom learning; the rest will become electronic credential mills. Those who graduate from online-propelled degrees may never enjoy a personal consultation with a professor.

With exceptions, online instruction reproduces on a grand scale the practice of many large public universities, where introductory courses typically enroll hundreds of students, who gather in a large auditorium to listen to a lecture by the professor, but are actually taught in sections led by graduate students employed as "teaching assistants." This type of instruction functions as a sorting device. Whether intentionally or not, it weeds out students who cannot make it in big classrooms, largely those with a low tolerance for boredom. They usually cannot ask questions of the professor, and often the section leaders do not know the answers. Some students who cannot tolerate mass education transfer to smaller schools; others drop out.

Returning adults who have not experienced a classroom environment since high school may find online classrooms more comfortable, because they do not require travel to a campus. But the question is,

What is learned in them? Does this style of pedagogy encourage reading and writing and peer interaction? If so, how? Does the student emerge from this experience with more autonomy, or does the instruction style promote rote learning? Most of the extant research focuses on cost benefit to the institution and convenience for the students, but rarely on the quality of the education they receive.

And higher education may prove to be a laboratory for a new universal educational regime. Already the conversation has begun: facing severe financial constraints, high schools and middle schools may soon be advised to adopt online programs, though at first only for science and math education. But once these programs begin, it might not be long before K–12 schooling is taken over by online teaching and learning.

Such an approach would be consistent with what Paulo Freire has termed the banking model of education, a model already broadly applied today in many schools. The model is based on several ideas about education:

1. Scientific knowledge is a done deal. That is, science has arrived at a series of truths in physics, chemistry, biology and other mainline sciences. Rote learning is the best way to transmit these truths to the student.

2. The student is ignorant, more or less—a blank slate. The task of education is to fill the student's brain with received wisdom.

3. In courses involving thousands or hundreds of thousands of students, online learning enables the system to enlist the most eminent authorities to deliver lectures on the latest discoveries or educational methods. Thus, the figure of the teacher is entirely replaced; however, genuine critical learning may be more limited, because the teacher is no longer primarily responsible for either the curriculum or the pedagogy. She has become a trainer.

4. Carrying this theory to its logical conclusion, we no longer need to issue so many PhDs or even master's degrees. Think of the savings.

5. If students can receive most of their education at home, we don't need so many school buildings, equipment and maintenance workers. Again, think of the savings.

It is true that the alternative, an intellectually rigorous curriculum taught according to the practice of dialogic pedagogy, which respects the learner as a producer as well as recipient of knowledge, has fallen on hard times. But this is no reason to submit to the dumbing-down that is now pervasive in much educational thinking. If online learning is likely to become a preferred method of delivering higher credentials, then we want to know how organized labor views it becoming a central component of schooling at all levels—a change that would affect union members, their children, and their communities. In general, the unions are mute on the issue, even though online schooling reproduces common industrial practices: knowledge and know-how are dictated from above, and the student is trained only as a future worker, not as an active participant in a democratic polity.

Most unions do not offer their members—let alone members' families—an educational program that asks questions about technology, specifically the question of how workers can transition from conventional industrial labor to professional and technical occupations. Nor do they address the pervasive problem of literacy among manual workers, where *literacy* is defined as the ability to grasp concepts, acquire the habits of reading and writing, and obtain numeracy. There are exceptions, such as New York's three centers for worker education at CUNY. Some 2,500 union members and labor activists at the centers are enrolled in a variety of associate's, bachelor's, and master's programs in the liberal arts and urban and labor studies. But as a rule the unions have given up their educational mission, including even steward's training in contract administration. Business unionism, the current standard orientation of American unions, is infected by an economism that avoids explorations of culture, housing, education, class and other aspects of the everyday lives of working people. The idea that technology, for instance, could be the subject of deconstruction and intellectual debate is far from the mentality of contemporary unionists, even those on the left. This avoidance is remarkable, considering that the massive devastation of the working class and its trade union sectors is not primarily a result of global migration but rather of technological displacement.

Adaptive and Interventionist Strategies for Addressing Technology

With few exceptions, American unions have historically focused their attention on the full-time worker. In the decades when organized labor was almost entirely a private-sector movement, the unions were selective about which categories of wage and salary workers were eligible for unionization. They concentrated first on skilled and semi-skilled employees who worked for wages in industrial production, construction, and service industries. Rarely, as they did for the auto industry in the Detroit area, the union recruited engineers and technical groups, and in the 1930s the CIO had an affiliate, the Federation of Architects, Chemists, Engineers and Technicians (FACET), that organized on both coasts, especially among technicians in the California oil industry and architects and engineers in smaller East Coast firms.[2] The CIO's Electrical Workers, also made sporadic attempts to organize salaried professional and technical workers, but most other unions in major production industries did not. The membership of the tiny American Federation of Technical Engineers was concentrated in relatively small workplaces. Even the UAW made no concerted effort to organize professionals in other auto, farm equipment, and aircraft industries.

Unwillingness to recruit professionals to the movement mirrors the unions' similar neglect of supervisory workers. The National Labor Relations Act excludes managers from the protection of the law, and so unions came to believe that "management" was their main adversary and that supervisory workers included in bargaining units during representation elections would naturally vote against unionization. Rather than fighting for the right of managerial workers to be organized, they approved, or were indifferent to, the NLRA's legal exception of them.

The labor federations were equally indifferent to the vast changes in the labor process that occurred in virtually every branch of industrial production. They tended to accept technological changes as inevitable and to adapt their collective bargaining strategies to them rather than attempting to bargain over the changes themselves, as the Steelworkers had once tried to do.[3] But in the 1960s, the Steelworkers abandoned the technology-review clause in the basic steel contract. Union leadership was convinced that the U.S. industry would be forced to match its European and Japanese competitors by adopting their job-destroying labor processes. The industry began replacing its outmoded equipment with computer-driven machines for most stages of the labor process. The changes dramatically increased worker productivity, reduced the workforce, and stabilized some of the sinking companies. But in the absence of federal protectionist policies, these adjustments came too late to spur a real revival of the industry.[4]

The boldest union adaptation to new technology was made by the West Coast's International Longshore and Warehouse Union (ILWU). The industry wanted to introduce containerization, an automated shipping and cargo-loading process that replaced most of the hand-loading that had defined longshore work for centuries. The proposal provoked an intense period of debate and disagreement. ILWU leadership was convinced that resistance to technological change would condemn the ports under their control to oblivion, that other countries, particularly Canada and Mexico, and their domestic rival, the Gulf Coast, would agree to containerization and the stevedore companies would shift West Coast work to those regions. So they demanded an unusual adaptation to the new technology: the company would adopt containerization, and qualified workers would be paid whether they worked or not. This quid pro quo was radical in its implications: for the first time in U.S. history, the workers were claiming a share in the enhanced profits of enterprise not as a bonus but as a right. Under the ILWU/Pacific Maritime Agreement, as long as employees in the "A" category reported for work, they were paid full salary, whether or not they were assigned to move cargo that day. The agreement also provided for a "B" category of employees not covered by the guaranteed wage. A similar deal was concluded by the International Longshoremen's Association (ILA), which represents workers on the East and Gulf Coasts.[5] The only parallel agreement can be found in the newspaper industry, where printers in the International Typographical Union (ITU), whose hand-typesetting skills were made obsolete by machines, were paid to take extended furloughs for as long as six months or more. But the pattern in other branches of industrial production was that unions simply conceded the usual layoffs. In some agreements, workers were offered severance pay if they accepted permanent displacement; in others, such as the Auto Workers', laid off employees with sufficient seniority on the job received full pay until they were offered a new job by the company. They were also allowed to refuse relocation to sites outside their residential area, but if they were offered transfers within their region they were obliged to accept them or lose their wage guarantees. The UAW Big Three and farm-equipment agreements have a "thirty and out" provision: a fifty-five-year-old worker can receive a pension after thirty years of employment. In 2000, the pension exceeded $3,000 a month. For those eligible for Social Security benefits, the retirement package has equaled their straight-time hourly earnings.

The issue raised by these developments is whether in a time of revolutionary technical change unions became the midwife of the abolition of industrial labor. Since the early 1960s more than half of the industrial work force has been eliminated, either by electronically controlled machinery or, in low-technology sectors such as apparel and small metal fabrication, by the export of jobs to developing countries like China, India, and Mexico. Unlike longshore, auto, and printing workers, most displaced employees have been forced to accept lower-wage jobs and in many instances to leave their homes, even their regions, in both the unionized and the nonunion private sectors.

As their members have literally been cast adrift, most unions have been unable to implement adaptive strategies. Unemployment benefits in almost all states are limited to twenty-six weeks and can only be increased by state and federal legislative action. The recent extensions of jobless pay reflect the government's tacit recognition that the current crisis is no longer cyclical but may last for another decade or more. Even so, Congress and most state legislatures restrict the amount and duration of unemployment coverage on the explicit assumption that we still have an economy that sees cyclical recessions and spurts of growth that produce relatively full employment. If the executive and legislative branches actually acknowledged the long-term, perhaps permanent nature of the crisis, there might be a debate about the need for a guaranteed income policy.

Worker Displacement Through Plant Migration Overseas

The migration of textile production abroad in the first decade of the twenty-first century has been a departure from the general pattern in that industry. Textile migration was previously within U.S. borders, and in 1997, the Amalgamated Clothing and Textile Workers (ACTW) had reason to be optimistic about its chances to organize the South, where the bulk of the almost million-worker industry had relocated. The union had recently organized six plants in the giant JP Stevens chain, largely in the upper South. Moreover, despite the low level of union organization, the industry had responded to global competition and growing union pressure by adopting computer-mediated labor processes. Bruce Raynor, the union's executive vice-president, an experienced Southern textile organizer, expressed confidence that the industry's technological modernization would deter most leading companies from moving offshore or to Mexico and other Latin American countries.[6]

Yet by the new century, most of the textile industry had already moved substantial fractions of production to China and India or were preparing their exit strategies, leaving dozens of one-industry textile towns bereft of viable sources of employment. The union was in no position to assist these mostly unorganized workers. Town and state governments, having subsidized a considerable portion of plant relocation from the Northeast and Midwest—building facilities and offering deferred taxes, free water and electricity, and the full cooperation of police forces and churches in discouraging unionization—were desperate to attract alternative businesses. Some have since been able to bring research firms to their communities, but most remain economically depressed. With cotton imports outselling domestic goods, sometimes by the practice of "dumping" at below market prices, the textile industry in the United States has been reduced to a relatively small number of cotton mills and a series of specialty manufacturers. In December 2012, the U.S. Bureau of Labor Statistics reported 119,900 total employees and 96,000 nonsupervisory workers in the industry, a reduction of about 80 percent of the 1980 labor force.

As unions have been unable (or unwilling) to either confront technology and its consequences or to find creative adaptive strategies, is it wildly utopian to ask what the role of the federal government might be in alleviating worker displacement and consequent suffering? It is not unusual for European governments to address technologically or globally induced unemployment. When the French government shut down much of its nationalized steel industry in the 1980s, it mollified workers and their unions by providing several years of income comparable to their employed wages in addition to training and education to assist them in finding alternative employment. In the United States, aside from our perennially contested unemployment compensation (which pays, typically, half of what workers earned when employed), federal efforts to address technologically or globally induced joblessness have been spotty. The 2013 limit to unemployment compensation was seventy-three weeks—not even a year and a half—in a period when there were almost 13 million officially unemployed.[7] If part-time and nonreporting discouraged workers had been factored in, that number would have been almost 26 million—15 percent of the total workforce. And even that figure does not account for the growing army of the underemployed—college-educated workers forced into the woefully precarious service sector, largely in restaurants.

The Failure to Organize the New Middle Class

The growth of the salaried middle class has not slowed since World War I. In the past century, administration has burgeoned. This rise of the bureaucracy marks not only the industrial goods–producing sector but also the service industries: sales, government, health care, education, the arts and even the trade unions. In the past two decades, the growth of the education and health bureaucracies has far outpaced the growth of those sectors' line labor. The college or university is no longer merely a place of teaching and learning; it has also become a dwelling for business administration graduates, whose job is to run the organization—its finances, services, grants, real estate, public relations, and public programs. And, to the extent that scientific and technical innovation have become the characteristic feature of production and services, the role of research and development has captured center stage, both at institutions of higher learning and in the industries their graduates populate and their research feeds. Research has now become the lifeblood of industry, providing new products, but more importantly, ever more labor-destroying technologies.

By the late 1950s, salaried white-collar and service employees outnumbered workers employed in industrial production. This phenomenon was not confined to the private sector: rapid expansion of public employment at the federal, state and local levels had created a vast new crop of clerical, professional, technical, and managerial workers and a smaller group of manual workers.

In December 2012, the Bureau of Labor Statistics recorded just over 8 million production workers. Also in 2012, BLS reported that some 17 percent of the labor force were office employees and 5 percent were professional and technical employees. This translates into more than 26 million office workers and nearly 8 million professional and technical employees. The private sector had about 22.5 million office workers and 6.5 million professional and technical workers, not counting service professionals in nonprofits. Adding nurses, physicians, and other health professionals brings the total to 11 million professional and technical workers, almost half as many workers as in the industrial sector. Include teachers, social service workers, and professors—both full- and part-time—and there are more than 16 million professional workers. In sum, the professions now account for about one in eight members of the labor force. Apart from the health and higher education professions and public school teaching, where the density of unionized labor is high (80 percent in the K–12 schools, 25 percent in higher education and health care), the organization of private-sector professional and technical employees and the overwhelming majority of office workers has been negligible.[8]

What these numbers tell us is that unions today do not speak for the whole working class, which includes the employed middle class, and that omission is killing the labor movement. Unions have organized only a narrow segment of workers in production, services, and public employment. It is not a question of lack of union density, where *density* signifies the proportion of union members in the overall workforce, but of a lack of breadth, of inclusion. It is the movement's limited diversity that makes it easier for labor's opponents to label the unions a pressure group that represents only its ever shrinking membership.

Yet the amount of pressure organized labor actually brings to bear on our political process and social policy making is much smaller than it could and should be. Here is where the American obsession with the importance of numbers, expressed in the term *union density,* with its majoritarian bias, must be challenged. The Tea Party's membership represents only a small fraction of the adult population and of the Republican Party. Yet the Tea Party speaks in a disproportionately loud voice, operating in the electoral arena by political threat in order to further its antitax program and "small" government message (which demands spending cuts in social programs but not in the military budget). It works within the Republican Party for its own ends and wields a strong influence over the GOP's agenda.

In contrast, the AFL-CIO is an appendage of the Democratic Party. It does not aggressively advocate for its agenda or threaten the DP's center-right elected majority, which for the past two decades has included its presidential administrations. The union may utter its disagreement with a given proposal, say, one to reduce Social Security benefits or cut Medicare, but it will not mobilize its forces to demonstrate against or boycott candidates who do not follow union lines, nor does it run genuinely pro-worker candidates in primaries, much less form a separate party. Obama's chief campaign consultant David Axelrod was telling the truth when he assured his listeners in the year leading up to the 2012 presidential elections that they need not "worry" about the left, including the unions. During that year the unions suspended criticism of the Obama administration and the left-liberals were mostly silent as well.

In short, labor today is not a movement, because it rarely, if ever, acts independently. Ever since the AFL-CIO decided to prioritize electoral politics over organizing and industrial action, it has made huge financial and activist contributions to the Democratic campaign, and yet workers' issues have been relegated to the margins of the DP agenda.

The French Direction

In France, the percentage of the private-sector workforce that is unionized is no greater than in the United States; however, French unions embrace a wider swath of those who work for wages and salaries and have historically spoken and demonstrated aggressively. French truckers have blocked public roads to call attention to their demands; French public workers have filled the streets of Paris to protest job and benefits cuts; French professors have struck against the proposed vocationalization of the university curriculum. French unions have fought for and won a system of industrial relations that allows any workforce of more than fifty employees to bargain collectively with its employer whether it is unionized or not. The works committee is the bargaining agent and it is elected by the employees of the entire enterprise.

Because France's three principal unions do not have exclusive representation or control over bargaining rights for workers, they must fight to elect their adherents to works committees. For most of the postwar era most of these committees were dominated by the Communist-led Confederation of Labor (CGT), but in recent years, as the Communist Party has lost political strength, they have been more diverse in composition.

This system based on competitive unions within a common workplace has kept the unions closer to the ground, although bureaucratic domination persists. But in recent months French unions have indicated their agreement with a proposal that would weaken the labor laws to permit employers to discharge workers and would install other changes that purportedly are necessary to make the French economy more competitive. Evidently the French now aspire to the labor market "standards" of the United States, where aside from some (effectually unenforced) protections against race and gender discrimination employers have few restraints over their control of the labor market. Even in some unionized workplaces—never mind the vast majority of nonunion private sector plants and offices—the power to hire and fire belongs exclusively to the boss. U.S. unions have agreed to two-tier wage systems and wage freezes and for the most part have not resisted the runaway shop. Under these pro-capital conditions, the U.S. labor market *is* competitive, and in recent years, in some goods production sectors, the United States has been a favored shop site for European and Japanese corporations.

Professional Employees in Charge of Industrial Production

Widening the reach of the unions is imperative in an era when constant technological change rules the workplace. Craftspeople and semiskilled operatives were once central to industrial production and services. Today, engineers, scientists, and managers control them, through computer and other electronically mediated technologies. This shift was recognized as early as 1921, in Thorstein Veblen's book *Engineers and the Price System*. Veblen said that the AFL—a craft-based federation—was doomed to marginalization; engineers were the key to the highly mechanized labor process. However, he held out little hope that engineers could be recruited into unions as long as capital was prepared to pay them handsomely. This judgment remains a challenge to unions, one they have been reluctant to take up. Of course, the typical goods-producing plant still employs manual labor. But semiskilled labor now operates machines, such as robots and computer consoles, that are designed and controlled by engineers and maintained by mechanics, who themselves have been reduced to being repair workers. In many factories, the "manual" worker is typically an observer of heat, velocity, and material flows. In effect, she has become a mere record keeper, because the machine that does the real work is relatively autonomous; it, not human labor, is the center of production. This is true of many processes in machine tools, chemicals, glass, plastics, food processing, and rubber and steel production.

To place the issue theoretically: We have embarked on an era when immaterial labor—the work of the brain rather than of the hands—is the cutting edge of industrial production and the services. Many workers in the service sector—waitpersons in restaurants, retail clerks, and public service employees—have jobs with manual and intellectual dimensions, just as engineers and scientists do who make some of their own tools or conduct experiments manually. The distinction between intellectual and manual labor is often social and ideological, not empirical. The problem is that neither organized labor nor labor theorists pay much attention to the content of immaterial labor or to its social and economic significance. Consequently, workers and their unions have effectively conceded control of the new labor process to company managers and owners. Their ability to intervene in it is limited; at best, they have devised adaptive strategies to deal with technological changes and, as we have argued, have increasingly worked themselves into a marginalized corner.

The conventional wisdom is that as long as money is the leading yardstick of labor relations, capital will always have the advantage. In the highly concentrated industries, wage demands could easily be accommodated, because capital, through its professional cadres, controls the conditions of production, distribution, and sales of the commodity. That a corporation such as Caterpillar has, for the past twenty years, successfully defeated strikes is not the result of global competition, but rather of the weakness of the labor movement. If unions raised the question of control, they would raise the odds of worker victories. Yet the issue has not been a major component of labor's demands. Pressed by home mortgages, car payments, and tuition, most workers have a hard time paying their basic bills. When the employer at the bargaining table offers signing bonuses in lieu of wage increases, or, worse, as compensation for long-term wage freezes, workers tend to grab them.

In the health care field, however, as doctors have increasingly become salaried employees rather than self-employed and nurses have played a more central role in the delivery of services to patients, the main grievances are no longer about income. Doctors and nurses are very interested in workplace control. They complain that administration has subverted their autonomy, that decisions concerning patients' health are no longer the exclusive province of the health professional. Treatment regimes are now handed down to them, often dictated from above. Management exercises control over issues of diagnosis, treatment—including choice of medication—and the organization of the professional's time. In effect, the doctor and the nurse have been reduced to functionaries of the health care machine. Needless to say, the practice of medicine is itself subject to *machines*—computers, electronic scans,

MRIs. It is also subject to the pressures of science as enterprise, in the drugs promoted to the hospital and the doctors by big pharmaceutical corporations.

Now that health care is managed by large organizations, some of them for profit, the once independent physician works under constant surveillance. Are these developments topics for union intervention? Where doctors have become unionized—about 15,000 in several organizations, most of them affiliated with the Service Employees—questions of autonomy are a theme of organizing drives. Yet once a drive is over, health care unions revert to making traditional trade union demands regarding salaries and benefits, even though for most doctors and, recently, registered nurses, physician's assistants, and nurse practitioners, these are not burning issues. The question of autonomy is, but doctors' and nurses' unions have not consistently raised it.[9]

On January 12, 2013, the *New York Times* reported on its front page that the New York Health and Hospitals Corporation, which operates eleven New York City public hospitals, was planning to implement a new program basing doctors' salaries on patient-care outcomes: "The proposal represents a broad national push away from the institutional model of rewarding doctors for the volume of services they order, a system that has been criticized for promoting unnecessary treatment."[10]

This proposal followed the Affordable Care Act's requirement for evaluating patient care by outcomes and cost containment. We observe the parallel between this proposal and the highly controversial practice, already in force in many cities and states, of basing teacher evaluations, at least in part, on student test scores. Plainly, these changes from past practices are dictated by the Obama administration's program to transform social services from a nonmarket-based system into a competitive results–oriented system based on market principles. There are two bottom lines here: cost containment and sharp limitation of intellectual and professional workers' autonomy through the transfer of decision-making power to management. These practices will change the relationship of medical professionals to their labor, to the institutions that employ them, and to the state. As labor issues, they include but go beyond concerns over salary and benefits, because they address the quality rather than the quantity of the service the worker is expected to provide.

Unions in the medical and educational sectors have little or no perspective on these questions. If they had, they would realize that opportunities for a real breakthrough in their organized power are being created by the very authorities who put the issue of control on the line by proposing outcomes assessment—whether test scores or treatment outcomes—as a primary means of evaluating salaries, employment and promotions.

It will take a relatively high degree of social understanding to address this subversion of brain workers' autonomy. When the Chicago teachers struck for more decision-making voice, the mayor offered money instead, because his administration understood the importance of retaining control. Apparently, the union was unprepared for a sustained fight over the control issues it had raised. The struggle would have exposed it to incredible scorn from politicians and the media; to overcome that would have required both a strongly unified labor movement and a deep alliance with parents and community organizations. The demand for more autonomy is unique in contemporary labor relations, and for any union to make it credibly will require a long period of preparation, public education, and both external and internal organizing. The union must also be prepared to resist its own national union's reluctance to take on such a fight. We will return in the last chapters to some of these problems. Suffice it to say for the present that the unions, which have given full-throated support to the Democratic Party and its candidates, now need to reexamine their relationship to Democratic public officials, who are among the main culprits when it comes to opposing power-sharing with public employees.

When Veblen wrote his epistle *The Engineers and the Price System* in 1921, engineers, in short supply, were just emerging from their tradition of self-employment to accept salaried positions. As the giants of industrial production—GE, Westinghouse, GM, Ford, and U.S. Steel, among others—actively recruited scientists and engineers, the main inducements they offered were economic. Later, during and after the World War II years, the development of electronically mediated communications brought a whole new cohort of scientific and technical professionals to corporations such as IBM, Kodak, Sperry Gyroscope, and the aircraft companies. During this period, discovery and invention were rewarded and for the most part were not subject to the vicissitudes of the economy. It was a time of war and cold war, and so funding for scientific and technical investigation was largely supplied by the government, which awarded contracts to private companies but owned the patents that derived from that research. After World War II, many of these patents were sold or given to the companies, which used them for private industrial purposes. Meanwhile, universities that had performed much of the science upon which the new technologies were based entered into their own "partnerships" with the companies: in return for research grants to academic departments, the university agreed to share or surrender the patents.[11] By the 1970s, the computer scientist and engineer were no longer independent entrepreneurs, but had become employees.

In the early days of the tech boom, IBM and other giant information corporations spun off a series of start-ups by advancing funding to some of their engineers, systems analysts, and programmers to develop personal computers. These "garage companies" were heralded by the mainstream media as evidence that small business was the heart of new-job creation. In time, the information giants either bought the patents for the inventions outright or shared in them with the inventors. There were, of course, some exceptions. Microsoft, Dell, and Google were self-started. As the personal computer business grew, a major union, the Communications Workers, attempted to organize Microsoft's Seattle professionals, but had little success, even though the company had just instituted a two-tier salary structure. The first tier enjoyed more or less secure employment and benefits but lower salaries than the precarious second tier, which had no benefits or job security at all.

The reason for this failure is that leading industrial unions were formed and remain based on traditional skilled and mass workers. By conceding the "qualified," credentialed intellectual worker to management, they have severely diminished their capacity for industrial action. As in the case of the oil industry, unless the engineers and managers of the technological industries are part of the union, any direct action except sabotage is impossible.

And the need for effective action and organized support from and among the professional working class will soon be urgent, for we can expect further spread of almost completely automated production processes in the near future. Such a regime is already in force in the production of oil, petro- and other chemicals, and engines, although not yet in vehicles production, which except for engine building is still only semi-automated. The development of automatic production is a major focus of corporate and university research, yet a perusal of union publications yields almost no information or discussion of this phenomenon and its implications for the labor movement. Nor is the problem of scientifically based technology in industrial production and the services a major concern of labor's militants, let alone its mainstream officials.

This lack of attention to science and technology is among the most revealing symptoms of "workerism" and other aspects of the failure of the imagination among unionists and their academic allies. Many union activists remain ensconced in old proletarian dreams inherited from the nineteenth and the first half of the twentieth century. Most academic labor historians and social scientists lock themselves into institutional studies rather than addressing the underlying social roots of the fate of labor.

Of course, to effectively question technology requires, first, a critical perspective on the development of capitalism, particularly the relation of technological change to profit rates and the social organization of labor, and, second, intimate knowledge of technology's scientific bases as well as how it works in specific spheres. Such knowledge, along with a thorough acquaintance with the history of the scientifically and technically based professions and the history of labor's experience with technology, would be absolutely necessary to the emergence of a labor movement rooted in the relations of production and contemporary labor processes. And we still need an informed history of labor's attempts to organize professionals in the private and public sectors.

Upping the Ante

There is yet another dimension to the evolution of almost all unions. We have already seen that, with few exceptions, labor education in the United States has atrophied. In addition, even the most "progressive" unions have ignored the everyday lives of their own members. The growth of mass unemployment in the first decades of the twenty-first century has been met by most unions with a deafening silence, except on the legislative plane. Even there, at best, the unions' political lobby has concentrated on maintaining unemployment benefits against the persistent attack on them from the right. There are practically no sustained efforts to organize the unemployed—union or nonunion—as a fighting force in labor struggles. Historically, it must be admitted, established unions have never mounted a real unemployed movement; that task was undertaken by the ideological left, mainly Socialists and Communists. In the dark days of the Great Depression, the Communist Party, the Socialist Party and the American Workers Party sponsored organizations of the unemployed; in the upsurges of 1933–37 these recruits played a role in organizing industrial workers and fighting for the introduction of jobless insurance at the federal and state levels. They also demonstrated in the cities against evictions, for relief from hunger and homelessness, and for jobs. Today, however, apart from small groups, there is no substantial organized left, and so the unemployed have been stranded.

There is no mass struggle—except by detachments of the Occupy Wall Street movement—against the millions of foreclosures, which mainly affect the working class, even many who are union members. And there is no effort to revive New York's innovative union-sponsored co-op housing, initiated by the Clothing Workers in 1927 and revived after World War II by the AFL Electrical Workers, the Ladies' Garment Workers, and Local 1199 of the Hospital Workers. In the main, today's unions have conceded housing to the real estate developers, landlords, and other private contractors. And with the almost sole exception of the teachers' unions, organized labor does not concern itself with the fate of its members' children in the public schools. Further, even though many children of union members and other working-class people have accumulated huge student debt, including in the once low-cost public colleges and universities, the fight to reduce or cancel such debt has been left almost solely to students themselves. Faculty in public universities seem reconciled to administration's tendency to raise tuition, which it does to make up for reductions the state legislatures impose on public spending for post-secondary schooling. It is worth noting here that because some unions participate in the horrendous credit-card industry and share in the proceeds with the banks and credit companies that sponsor their cards, they are seriously compromised on the issue of debt bailouts.[12]

The exclusive workplace orientation of most unions and their rank-and-file activists also contributes to their abandonment of the working class and salaried middle class to the financial institutions that control housing, are bidding to control education in many communities, and constitute the economic basis of a consumer culture that has operated to bankrupt large sections of the population. This is among the major shortcomings of both business unionism and its ideological rival, syndicalism. Although the workplace was once the necessary and sufficient condition for the growth and power of the labor movement, unions can no longer afford to ignore workers' everyday life or their relationship to the institutions that oppress them outside the workplace. For example, in a society in which housing has mainly evolved into single- or two-household units, in a boom-and-bust economy a mortgage crisis becomes inevitable.

Of course, the question now is whether the economy will boom again in the foreseeable future. With good reason, many people have come to doubt that the era of good jobs for people without technical training will return. For these people, schooling, the road to middle-class credentials, is the preferred insurance against economic ups and downs. But this is a dubious bet at a time when job creation is concentrated in the services, especially restaurants and big-box retailers and when full-time employment is either nonexistent or contingent. Retail food services employs a total of more than 9.3 million workers, making it the largest private-sector industry in the country. The 60 million workers in all service sectors now account for about 40 percent of the nation's workforce. At this moment, too, the country's largest employer, the combined public sector, is cutting workers. One of its oldest services, the post office, may soon be privatized, and the postmaster general has proposed cutting Saturday letter delivery.

In the private sector—aside from health care, which is generally nonprofit and hires a large number of credentialed workers—most new "jobs" are contingent, part-time and temporary. This is the other side of technologically created intellectual labor. For those who do not possess technical skills, the college degree has become less reliable as a ticket to stable, long-term employment. But even some trained scientists are condemned to contingency, their employment opportunities often confined to postdoctoral fellowships in large research organizations, mostly universities. These production workers of scientific and technological research are typically contract employees. Their contract lasts as long as their current project; when that is done, they must scramble to find another senior researcher willing to hire them. Since tenure-track professorships are scarce, postdoc fellowships have in effect become a career. If the fellows are fortunate they may eventually find an academic job in a community college or a third-tier four-year school. Otherwise, they remain contingent contract laborers, members of the precariat.

The Occupy Wall Street movement drew significant numbers of college and university graduates who had found that their credentials earned them not the promised career but instead work (hardly what we call a job in the traditional sense) in a restaurant or department store. This work typically does not offer full-time hours, and the pay is at or close to minimum wage, except in the higher-end restaurants, which are by definition relatively few in number. There, too, only minimum wage is guaranteed, but tips are mostly generous, and a server's income may range from $600 to more than $1,000 a week, but only if the server is called in for five full shifts. Entry-level department store labor pays slightly above the federal minimum and offers less than full-time assignments. For most of Walmart's 1.1 million employees, the workweek is twenty-four hours at $8–$9 an hour. There is no guaranteed shift. Workers are called one to three hours before a shift. Those who receive no call cannot report for work. It is not unusual for a worker to hold two such jobs, one at Walmart or Target, and another at McDonald's, Burger King, or a similar fast-food restaurant for more or less the minimum wage and few or no tips.

In fall 2012 several thousand Walmart workers—including those in one of the company's major distribution centers outside Chicago—struck in protest against the store's labor policies. Some of the inside organizers were political activists, but significantly, most of the strikers were uncredentialed working poor. Among these were single mothers, who joined the picket lines despite worries about being fired and unable to pay their bills.[13]

The strikers did not seek union recognition or expect to win a collective bargaining agreement. Their aim was to call attention to the substandard wages and working conditions in the largest U.S. corporation and to expose a benefits program that required workers to contribute a substantial portion of their meager wages. Their campaign was sponsored and funded by the United Food and Commercial Workers (UFCW), a 1.3 million–member affiliate of the loose federation Change to Win, a breakaway from the AFL-CIO organized principally by the Service Employees. UFCW's membership includes workers in packinghouses, chemical firms, and retail food and department stores. It holds collective bargaining agreements with Macy's, Bloomingdale's, and major West Coast and Northeastern supermarket chains, especially in Los Angeles, New York, and Philadelphia.

Walmart is the direct and formidable competitor of the union supermarkets and some department stores, and the union's motive in organizing minority movements against its policies may be to protect the wages and benefits of already unionized workers and the competitive position of their employers. But if the campaign is serious and does not founder on worker fear in our depressed economy, if direct action can succeed in raising wages and improving working conditions at the biggest big box, the impact on the industry could be even more substantial.

The 2012 Walmart actions were followed by parallel strikes at a McDonald's store in midtown Manhattan and at Wendy's, Burger King, and KFC. Hundreds demonstrated at Grand Central Station, in protest against poverty wages that rarely exceeded $10 an hour, and demanded a wage of $15 an hour. These actions were coordinated by Communities for Change and did not have visible trade-union backing. Fast food is a more widely dispersed industry than department stores or supermarkets. The typical McDonald's, Wendy's, Subway, or Burger King restaurant has fewer than fifteen employees. The strikes were simply for higher wages; they were not a demand for union recognition.

Two of New York's older worker organizations have taken similar steps without actually seeking union contracts. The 15,000 members of the Taxi Workers' Alliance have devoted more than a decade to upgrading the drivers' wages and working and living conditions, without engaging in collective bargaining. They have blocked traffic on Grand Central Parkway and the New York–area airports, picketed the Taxi and Limousine Commission offices, and staged strikes. Domestic Workers United, founded in 2000, has possibly the hardest road of any of the organizations of low-wage contingent workers. Consequently it focuses its efforts on education, such as training in household management and other job skills, and on fighting for protective legislation for its mostly Caribbean members, who often have immigration-status problems, including deportation.

In many cities, workers' centers are cropping up to fill the vacuum created by the indifference of established unions and political parties to the needs of immigrants and the industrial and service precariat. These centers are community-based and operate outside the system of collective bargaining. In 2010, there were more than 130 workers' centers, some serving mostly day laborers, some low-wage workers generally, and some the unemployed. By 2013 there were 274. The centers address a wide variety of issues: subminimum wages; unpaid labor, in which the employer fails to pay for regular time worked or else forces employees to work overtime without compensation; sexual harassment; discriminatory discharges; and unattended medical problems. New York's Restaurant Opportunities Center offers classes to workers seeking to upgrade their skills. Some centers have opened informal hiring halls that supply labor to employers willing to offer standard pay and conditions. Some provide referrals and other services to their constituents. Others, however, have been more militant, supporting strikes and job actions—not for the purpose of gaining recognition or contracts, but to oppose and change oppressive employer behavior. The centers' relations with the established unions vary from place to place. Their dealings with government agencies usually involve issues of enforcement: of fair wages, reasonable hours, and safety laws for the protection of the working poor.

Recently, some of the established unions have shown sympathy with and support for the idea of organizing the precariat and other working poor; however, the fate of millions of low-paid service workers remains on the margins of organized labor's agenda. In an era when with few exceptions jobs for the academically and technically unqualified are concentrated in the service industries, labor's failure to address the needs of low-paid contingent, part-time, and temporary workers goes against labor's avowed historical mission: to bring the most exploited workers as well as the most skilled to full industrial and social citizenship. The AFL-CIO and Change to Win leaders sometimes invoke "the death of the middle class" when Congress and employers refuse to address poverty and unemployment, yet the unions are not on the front lines for either employed scientists and technical formations or for the growing mass of the working poor.

CHAPTER SIX

Toward a New Labor Movement, Part One

How do we create a new labor movement able and willing to address the burning questions affecting workers today? As we have seen, American unions now confine themselves to workplace issues such as job security, benefits, and individual grievance fights and operate mostly within the collective bargaining agreement. With few exceptions, they have surrendered the strike weapon and other forms of direct action. They take part in electoral politics, but they do not use their political influence to tackle social issues like housing, education, food prices, consumer debt, or the debacle of soaring student debt. Just as they rarely fight the employers directly, they almost never demand that the Democrats they support adhere to labor's agenda. Instead, they have adopted a stance of cooperation and have been integrated into the economic and political status quo. In brief, few unions view themselves as responsible for the totality of workers' lives, even those of their own members and member households. Nor do they see themselves as an independent economic and political force.

The burden of my analysis is that the current unions are, in the main, incapable of and unwilling to make the radical shift necessary to convert themselves from service organizations into a fighting force that takes on power in its many dimensions. Further, they are not prepared to offer workers and the larger public an alternative to the prevailing setup. They are imprisoned within the legal and imaginative limits imposed by the largest corporations and the state on permissible activity and ideo-logical orientation. I have argued that the major obstacle is not their shrinking numbers. The slide in union membership is a symptom, not the cause, of a much larger problem. At the risk of contradicting conven-tional wisdom, which ascribes labor's decline to its nefarious opponents on the right and some of the large corporations, or to globalization, my starting point is to ask, What are the components of a vital social and political movement?

Genuine social movements arise when a social formation can no longer realize its aspirations for the good life in the prevailing system and are prepared to travel the arduous path of social transformation.[1] Historically, movements that cease to expand and improve and under adverse economic and political conditions are likely to stagnate and decline. Samuel Gompers's "More" may have served the AFL's craft union members adequately for the first decades of the twentieth century, but neither he nor his comrades in leadership considered the aspirations of the industrial workers or the possibility that changing economic, tech-nological, and political conditions might affect the crafts. In the 1930s, industrial workers were inspired by the idea that the union was a way to achieve industrial citizenship—that workers could get off their knees and out from under an imperial ownership that watched and controlled them on and off the job and dictated the terms and conditions of their employment and their lives. These workers sought to take their fate into their own hands. Just as workers had at the turn of the twentieth century, they brandished their desire for dignity in every strike, workplace occu-pation, and march through city streets. Their vision was not typically anticapitalist, but industrial unionism was a movement of a class that aspired to power over their own labor in the factory and other work-places at least, and in many instances also in their cities and towns. Union members ran for city council, were elected to school boards, and made their voices heard on a wide range of public policies.[2]

Today, U.S. unions have lost any semblance of this radical imagina-tion, and so are generally unable to inspire working-class passion. They have been passive in the face of dramatic changes in the economy, which have visited hardship on a considerable portion of the workers, and accepted the indifference of the political class to their problems. Their explicit commitment to the existing setup, particularly to the capitalist economic system, and to a perverse version of class peace, have put most of them in a dependent and defensive position. Specifically, they have no tools for any analysis that would help workers evaluate the state of their own affairs and those of the country at large. Dimly, unions recognize that we live in an age when national borders no longer define the economy, but they are still tied to conceptions of reform that this new age has outmoded. More egregiously, instead of acting for themselves, they have fixed their hopes on a series of political "saviors" who either ignore the needs of their labor allies or else pay them lip service and then proceed to betray their trust at almost every turn.

Compare union passivity to some of the leading social movements of the recent past. Members of the black freedom movement of the 1960s and '70s demanded full equality: in employment and wages, education, access to public accommodations, and electoral politics. They dared to question the freedom of a society that falsely claimed that all citizens were equal. They made public the widespread perception among blacks that although slavery had been abolished, they were not free. Freedom meant something more than formal equality under the law, although achieving formal rights was part of their struggle. Black freedom meant, first of all, social and political power, a truth first held self-evident by Marcus Garvey, Hubert Harrison, and other nationalists and the communists in the 1920s and 1930s, and again in the 1960s by Malcolm X and the Black Panthers.

The black power movement foundered on police terror and the limits imposed on blacks and other discriminated groups by a civil rights establishment that shrank in the face of corporate and union resistance to genuine economic equality and settled for legal rights and affirmative action. It is often forgotten that affirmative action was introduced by the Nixon administration to forestall demands for a broadly upgraded educational system and rigorous enforcement of antidiscrimination employment laws. But affirmative action failed to reach the overwhelming majority of blacks and Latinos, many of whom were and remained trapped in poverty.[3] The tacit purpose of the programs was to create a black middle class of salaried technical and administrative employees and, at a time of rebellion in the streets, a new coterie of politicians able to control black communities. To confront the power elite—corporate and political—would have entailed a level of ideological clarity and mobilization that the movement's leadership was unable—or not sufficiently prepared—to provide. Many leaders were content to accept the restrictions imposed by white liberal politicians and judges, who granted some social and educational gains to blacks who possessed enough cultural capital to qualify for higher education.[4]

Yet the movement did have people who proposed a new egalitarian vision, a new way of life for blacks, a vision that propelled mass protests that forced the enactment of the Voting Rights Act and Civil Rights Act, the antipoverty program, and a major shift in the public's perception of what a human right is. After the protests of the 1960s, many who had been in the vanguard of movement were awarded a place in the established order and settled for incremental changes, most of which, like affirmative action programs, helped expand the black middle class. On the premise that progress could be made from inside the established order, a significant fraction of the most militant activists sought and won elective office: they became mayors, state legislators, Congresspeople, and judges. Malcolm X, Fred Hampton of the Panthers, and Martin Luther King had been murdered when they proposed the radical shift from seeking equal rights to seeking equal power. These atrocities served as a warning to those who would transgress the limits of acceptable protest.

Similarly, when the feminist movement emerged in the late 1960s, its leading edge was radical: women who called attention to equality in the household, the bedroom, the workplace, education, and sports. Organizations like Red Stockings and Radical Women directly challenged the idea of patriarchy, the sexual division of labor that forces many women to perform both paid and unpaid (that is, household) labor. That radical effort was undercut by liberal feminists, who diverted much of the movement's activities to supporting the Democratic Party, contesting the glass ceiling in corporate boardrooms, and insisting on middle-class affirmative action. Nevertheless, one terribly important battle was won with the 1973 Supreme Court ruling on *Roe v. Wade*. The legal right to abortion has suffered evisceration in the last forty years, but the radical feminist demand that women have the right to control their own sexuality and their bodies was a huge cultural victory that has far outweighed the legal and legislative wins. Even though women are still paid, on average, 20 percent less than men for the same work, the relationship between men and women is not the same as it was before 1968. Although sexism has not disappeared, in the workplace or in the home, even women who refuse to call themselves feminists are imbued with a certain self-confidence, one that belies utterances such as "I'm no women's libber . . ." and, of course, that disclaimer is often followed by "*but . . .*"

The feminists had defined the good life in terms of women's autonomy, and the right knows it, knows they succeeded, and has never ceased to attempt to turn the clock back. The right knows, more clearly than most of the left or the liberals, that cultural space is one of the key battlegrounds. In fact, cultural reaction has become the signature of the Republican Party, and fortunately at the national level it has so far failed miserably. But as the GOP has taken political power at the state level, abortion rights, as they were in the 1992 ruling on *Planned Parenthood v. Bob Casey*, have been watered down, though not rescinded. Bob Casey was the Democratic governor of Pennsylvania, and the case was a challenge to legislation enacted during his terms in office requiring, besides three other restrictions, that a wife notify her husband and a daughter obtain her parents' permission in order to obtain an abortion. A narrow plurality on that era's conservative Supreme Court upheld a wife's right to privacy but let the other restrictions stand. Yet mainstream liberals persist in believing that the Democrats will protect feminist achievements, though as the right intensifies its onslaught, Democratic politicians defensively repeat the futile mantra of family values, a conservative slogan that has never served the goal of freedom.

Blacks and women in the 1960s and '70s won what they did because they were able to imagine what the good life would be and what they would need to achieve it. Without such a conception, beleaguered social formations must confine themselves to defending past gains. The U.S. unions have done worse: they have conceded many of their material gains to capital in the hope of preserving their institutional arrangements, the union contract and members' income that sustains it. They accept the prevailing setup—capitalism in the economy, legalism and electoralism in politics, and the sanctity of the contract in the workplace.

A better conception of the good life is essential if labor is to become once more a vital movement and force for social change. In the first place, that vision would provide the impetus for popular mobilization and recruit enough workers ready to take the risks without which the forward march is impossible. When the labor movement stood for human emancipation as well as higher living standards, its constituents were often willing to lay their jobs and even their lives on the line, because the unions promised a completely new way of life and of being. People who had been imprisoned by wage slavery and managerial domination saw that they could finally be free.

Today, workers have lost the idea that they can control the terms of their labor, that they need not force themselves to work underpaid and under intolerable conditions, that they can live free to give range to their imagination, to use their genuine talents, even to be lazy. Without that idea, their motivation to fight has been significantly reduced. Seventy-five years after the New Deal, organized labor has become a set of institutions that see nothing on the furthest horizon but the preservation of the New Deal's withered remains on the one hand, and on the other the all-but-eclipsed promise that workers can achieve higher living standards through collective bargaining.

What different vision could be on that horizon that would make the American working class willing to resume its march? For workers, the good life must begin with a substantial reduction of working hours with no reduction of pay, which would create jobs. More important, if shorter hours freed workers from the oppressive regime of brain-and-bone-numbing work without end, it would open the new vista of a life not only better but also fundamentally changed. We are living in an era when wage labor—getting it and keeping it—dominates everyday life. As real wages have fallen, the forty-hour workweek no longer supports many working-class families or even individuals. Both partners must work to pay household bills, or one must take a second job, leaving little time for anything else. And when overtime is offered them, they cannot—or dare not—refuse it.

In 2013 half of U.S. households reported having trouble making ends meet, and that is an egregious scandal in the richest country in the world. We tolerate an unprecedented concentration of our wealth in the hands of the few even as living standards for most of us continue to decline. Major reasons for this misplaced tolerance are the sorry state of the unions, the dread of unemployment that grips large sections of the population, and the virtual disappearance of individuals and institutions willing to fight for the fulfillment of working people's economic needs. For example, when extended benefits for the long-term unemployed were terminated at the turn of 2014, the labor movement did nothing beyond lobbying Congress to reverse the decision. What if, instead, they had mobilized the jobless to take direct action?

There are no effectively enforced labor rights in the United States today. Courts brazenly support employer demands for antistrike injunctions, while employers freely intimidate workers on the job, especially those seeking union recognition; routinely violate the laws enacted to protect workers' wages and hours; and engage in outright wage theft—all because they know that the federal and state governments are lax in enforcement, or else do not have the budget to do their jobs properly. Clearly, it is time to for labor to stop relying solely on workers' rights and begin relying more on workers' power. Power is the root of the matter. The question is: Power to do what?

First, workers who understood their own power could fight to reduce working hours, by pushing for new legislation and by taking direct action in the workplace. Instead of waiting for the Democratic Party to enact changes, unions could shake off their fear and complacency, unite, and launch a militant, long-range campaign like labor's first fight for shorter hours at the turn of the twentieth century—a battle fought with strikes, demonstrations, and agitation. These tactics were abandoned by the AFL in the early 1930s, as soon as the Roosevelt administration was willing to sponsor modest restrictions on hours; the real fight was led not by the official big unions but by radical political parties; shop and neighborhood committees; and militant minority unions. It was they who conducted the education and agitation, and they supported the legislative initiatives, such as the 1932 six-hour bill of Senator Hugo Black of Alabama, a bill that actually passed in the Senate, though it was ultimately blocked in the House by Secretary of Labor Frances Perkins. The eight-hour day was won originally by workers who knew and used their power. It has since been nearly lost, but it could be won again the same way.

Second, labor could fight for a guaranteed basic income. In recent years a group of economists and other intellectuals have made the proposal for one. Lacking a political base, the proposal has gained little traction, but the group, BIG (Basic Income Guarantee), has sponsored annual conferences and performed much of the research needed to put the concept on the political map. A new labor movement is needed to give muscle to their work. The struggle for the basic income guarantee is an urgent one, for the days of "full employment" (the term for 3 percent unemployment) are long gone. A jobless present and future may affect as much as 25 percent of the U.S. population by 2020. The United States is not bereft of the resources to pay for guaranteed income, but this solution has been ignored, thwarted, or refused consideration by mainstream politicians and economists who believe, wrongly, that an economic upturn that will deliver nearly full employment is just around the corner. Some even argue that income guarantees would prevent economic growth. Progressives like Paul Krugman and Joseph Stiglitz rely on Keynesian stimuli such as work programs to buttress income and overcome the current economic stagnation. Undeniably, the New Deal's work programs reduced unemployment, but they did not reverse mass unemployment. That distinction belongs to the war that devastated most of Europe and put the United States in a uniquely dominant economic hegemony for fifteen years of the postwar period. But mass unemployment has returned: today 25 million people are either jobless or underemployed, even as the president and his administration confidently declare that the economy is on the mend and depression and recession are conditions of the past.

Krugman and a few other liberal economists do not buy the Obama line. They declare that the United States is in depression, but while calling for a jobs program they have not raised the urgent need for shorter hours and a guaranteed income, measures that would naturally create more jobs. This is the task of the left, especially the labor left. As long as technological innovations in goods production, services, and the professions are oriented to reducing the role of labor, eliminating jobs and replacing full-time employment with precarious, part-time work, joblessness and poverty are going to increase and become permanent in the structure of the workplace and the labor market.

In his 2013 State of the Union address, Obama did ask Congress to raise the minimum wage to $9 an hour from its pitiful current rate of $7.25.[5] It should be noted that the fall 2012 strikes by low-wage fast-food workers demanded a minimum wage of $15 an hour. Although Obama has declared that no full-time worker should earn poverty wages, his proposal would leave millions below the poverty line, which is drawn considerably below an income level able to sustain a minimum level of comfort. Even $15 an hour is only $600 a week for forty hours of labor. In the largest cities, this sum does not leave much slack for workers who must buy their own health care insurance, pay a high rent or mortgage, maintain a car, and cover college tuition for themselves or their children. It only begins to approach a living wage. Here as elsewhere progressives are far too ready to hail any slight improvement that the liberal center is prepared to offer; they are afraid to push leftward for a genuine change lest instead of modest wins they get nothing. The labor left would have to look past the workplace to leap into the opening provided by Obama's statement; to act independently in the public sphere; to risk the usual liberal criticism that the radicals are ruining the workers' chance for improvement. Yet it was the Black bill, the left's campaign for shorter hours, and the industrial workers' upsurge of 1934 that prodded Franklin Roosevelt to shift from his 1932 pledge to balance the budget to the creation of the WPA, CCC, and other jobs programs and the legislation protecting wages and hours that was enacted in 1938.

Shorter hours, guaranteed income, and a higher minimum wage are serious structural reforms because they redistribute a portion of the wealth while helping to address the problems associated with economic stress and technological change. But shorter hours and guaranteed income alone are fairly passive strategies for adapting to the effects of technological change. A new labor movement would also have to devise strategies to intervene in the *process* of technological change, to demand control over its introduction and design, and a say in how the product is made. It would play a role in constructing a new division of labor that does not relegate workers to boring, repetitive operations, that affords them a creative role in developing new methods of producing goods and services. And these proposals are not meant for U.S. labor alone:

the moment for workers of the world to answer the *Manifesto*'s call and rise together to fight their oppression has come.[6]

Third, the new labor movement must address workers in terms of the totality of their lives rather than exclusively as wage earners: join the educational debates raging throughout the country; take on the crisis in housing, of which foreclosure rates are merely the tip of the iceberg; raise hell about the virtually closed-down state of mass transit; and challenge the powerful cultural apparatus that monopolizes much of our free time and fosters illusions about the reality of the American Dream.[7] Up to now there have been few signs that unions are willing or even able to engage—let alone intervene—in these issues. That has to change. In the cities of the Northeast and West Coast, the movement must confront spiraling rents that are driving the working class—employed or not—from the cities. Henri Lefebvre has written that ordinary people have the "Right to the City" against the real estate barons and the banks that relentlessly pursue gentrification. Instead of moving up, workers are moving out.[8] In New York, Boston, Los Angeles, and San Francisco, college-educated young people occasionally protest high rents and foreclosures, because as members of the growing urban precariat, they, too, are victims of gentrification, paying exorbitant rents or mortgages out of poverty wages—which also makes them gentrifiers. Those who cannot afford to live alone or even with a partner cram with friends into small apartments. Latinos, African-Americans, and working-class whites with children are deprived of the pleasures of urban living entirely, even though the work they find is often in the city. Obviously, the dearth of affordable city housing is a labor issue, but the unions mostly ignore it.

Public schools are another: those in working-class neighborhoods are almost always of poor quality. Facilities are underfunded and the school buildings often dilapidated; teachers are disaffected because they must manage overcrowded classrooms, teach to standardized tests, and bring work home almost every night. The charter schools in these districts are publicly funded but privately run. They are invariably heralded by school authorities as educational models, but they have not proved to be qualitatively better than their public counterparts. Yet the media cherry-pick for discussion the few that are, and legislatures hurry to authorize more funds to expand their number. The teachers' unions accurately claim that they drain already reduced resources from public schools, but their voices are drowned out by the hype. It should not fall only to the teachers to challenge the crisis in public education, but most unions, preoccupied with their own survival, are simply not players in the struggle. Workers in factories, service industries, construction, and the public sector must rely on parents' associations—which are often colonized by school administrators—to voice their concerns; there are no real parents' unions to defend and extend their interests by direct action. Yet in the past twenty years schooling has become a labor issue: credentials are the first qualification for the new high-tech workplaces and for entrance into the burgeoning army of administrative workers. Yes, more working class students today do enter some institution of higher education. But the dropout rate is appalling, because most of these students are forced to work full-time to pay tuition and support themselves or contribute to the family income.

Fourth, the new labor movement must take seriously the question of workplace democracy. Workplace democracy, realized in ideas such as workers' control, has never taken hold in mainstream U.S. labor circles. Of course, union democracy, which the rank and file have a certain measure of power to put into effect, has been the focus of recent radical movements within the unions. The main problem with workers' control is the perspective from which it has been introduced. In the past quarter-century, workers have been invited by capital to "participate" in the management of the enterprise. Activists have correctly characterized such programs as company unionism and class collaboration. Participation has often meant workers being encouraged to give ideas for improving their own productivity. The long-term result has been worker co-option rather than increased worker power. When, reluctantly, unions have gone along with corporate participation schemes, they have rarely proposed their own program, one that would allow workers to actively intervene in workplace decisions. This reticence may reflect unions' respect for management prerogatives as well as an actual fear of getting too deeply involved in company decision making. Such involvement might lead to conflict, a mode from which many union leaders now recoil. Instead, they have permitted the company to set the terms and conditions of participation and have reserved only the workers' right to grieve. It is worth noting that unions have not made the issue of worker control part of the bargaining process, internal education, or their political program. They remain in a reactive stance.

But as we have seen, if workers and their unions fail to intervene in certain questions, notably the introduction of new technology, their power is significantly diminished, their jobs disappear, and in most cases they can find no equivalent jobs to replace them. Yet since the 1970s, as capital has migrated to the American and global south, there has been little protest, resistance, or union intervention.

Workers elsewhere have found another solution to capital migration. In Argentina, beginning at the turn of this century, when employers closed down pottery factories, workers occupied the plants and resumed production. The bosses, though they had no intention of reopening the factories themselves, put pressure on the government to remove the workers. After prolonged struggles, some workers have been forced to vacate their plants, but many others have effectively defended their initiative and kept the factories open. On February 12, 2013, workers in Greece reopened a closed building materials factory and began to manage it themselves. Their main obstacle has been the refusal of banks to extend loans, but the workers are still operating the factory and are determined to make it a success. There are self-managed factories in Spain under the coordination of Mondragon, and a self-managed factory has been established in Egypt. There are even a few examples of recent factory occupations in the United States. In December 2008, members of the United Electrical Workers responded to the closure of a Chicago window factory by occupying it. They demanded and got severance pay from the company and have considered operating the plant on a cooperative basis, although they have not yet been able to take that step.

But in general in the United States, workplace occupations, which were vital in the industrial union upsurge of the 1930s but were made illegal by a Supreme Court decision in 1938, have all but vanished from labor's arsenal. Nor has organized labor looked beyond its acceptance of the prevailing private ownership–driven system for the production of goods and services. In the 1970s and 1980s, during airline bankruptcies and plant closings, employees began agreeing to participate in Employee Stock Ownership Plans (ESOPS), to save their jobs and help refund the companies. But the vast majority of these plans gave workers no role in controlling production or services. Their union representatives sat on boards of directors, but facilities were subject to professional management and the wage-labor relationship was unchanged from the days of private ownership. Some of these ESOPS have survived into the new century, and in some instances workers have benefited from profit sharing. But since the deepening of the economic crisis, profits in many of the small and medium-sized enterprises are thin. In other cases, for example that of United Airlines, once the company became profitable again, it was returned to private hands.

Farmers in the United States have long formed producer cooperatives to prevent large financial and processing firms from subordinating them. They have operated granaries and distribution companies and provided their own insurance. This tradition has been weakened over the years, but it is still alive. But workers' producer cooperatives with a real voice over company decisions are few and far between. Since capital has increasingly outsourced many areas of production to contractors at home and abroad and industrial and other employers are being replaced by financial corporations that prefer to move money rather than goods and services, the time has come for employees to consider taking control of their working lives by taking control of a workplace. Of course, like members of the U.S. farmers' co-ops and the Argentine workers' factories, they would still have to grapple with the market and with global technologies and methods of production, but at least they would have jobs. More important, they would begin to experience what it means to have the power of daily decision making.

What does a group of workers need to do to establish a self-managed workplace? Their first task is to raise the capital they will need to renovate the plant or office, to construct a payroll that anticipates months, even a year, of small profits or none, and to pay various charges, such as workers' compensation and contributions to state unemployment compensation funds. Could union pension funds provide this initial capitalization? In this regard it is worth noting that many of these funds are invested in the biggest polluting corporations, financial companies, and foreign imperial investors. A portion of profits from these enterprises supports the pensions that retiring workers will need to supplement meager Social Security checks, which is why many unions are reluctant to invest pension funds in moderate income housing or cooperative businesses, even though those businesses benefit workers more than the big corporations.[9] If producers' co-ops were to become a major labor program, this issue would take on a different urgency.

A Personal History of the Cooperative Solution

When my mother's family came to the United States in flight from Russia, they worked in men's and women's apparel factories. My great-uncle, a sewing machine operator, was a founder of the cloak makers' union, and a great uncle by marriage was an active member of the dressmakers' union. My grandfather was a skilled tailor and worked as a cutter in a men's suit factory. When these men entered the industry, the two apparel unions had already been organized in some major cities, including Chicago and New York. Both the International Ladies' Garment Workers' Union (ILGWU) and the Amalgamated Clothing Workers of America (ACW) were led by socialists, and most of the Jewish and Italian workers in the industries were either socialists or anarchists. From its formation in 1900 to 1936 ILGWU was aligned with the Socialist Party and so was the ACW, which had formed in 1913 as a split-off from the AFL's United Garment Workers. The ACW and ILGWU pioneered union-sponsored health care centers and consumer co-ops, and in the late 1920s, the Amalgamated built housing co-ops on the Lower East Side and in the North Bronx. My great-aunt's husband, after working in the garment shops, became a labor journalist for the Jewish *Daily Forward*. The couple had an apartment in the Bronx co-op and so did my grandfather. In the 1930s, on Allerton Avenue in the East Bronx, a Communist-sponsored cooperative housing development was built. This one failed to maintain its co-op status but remained a haven for assorted left-wing workers who stayed as renters.

These were true housing cooperatives with strict rules for shared ownership, not the expensive enterprises called co-ops today, which allow members to resell their apartments to the highest bidder. The unions sponsored them as part of their commitment to provide decent affordable housing at a time when masses of workers lived in tenements, built by the real estate industry and deliberately designed to be slums. The tenements' poor quality and crowded conditions had created problems that the real estate investors were unable or unwilling to solve. The unions believed that only the labor movement could address workers' needs and that housing should be top of the list.

Their co-ops were built and maintained on a nonprofit basis and offered an alternative not only to tenement conditions but also to the landlord-tenant relationship.

When my parents moved into the Bronx Amalgamated co-op in 1952, they bought their two-bedroom apartment for less than $3,000. Their neighborhood grocery store was a supermarket sponsored by the socialist-leaning Eastern Consumer Cooperatives.[10] And believing that workers need roses as well as bread, cultural enrichment along with housing, the Bronx co-op provided very inexpensive child-care services, cultural institutions, and an educational program.

When my mother died in 2010, she had been living for thirty-eight years on West 25th Street in Manhattan, in Penn South, where she moved some years after my father's death in 1967. Penn South began as an ILGWU-sponsored housing co-op. Like Bronx Amalgamated, it offered lectures and other educational events; it also had a social services department that addressed co-op members' personal financial and social problems. The co-op movement tried to address the whole person, beyond simple economic issues.

By the 1970s the union co-ops had become a part of a nonprofit housing organization called Mutual Housing and Development. In 2010, my mother was paying $510 a month in maintenance fees, which included a small sum to cover the cost of cogeneration in the 10,000-person complex, but no rent. By then, her $3,000 investment had grown to $13,000, but under co-op rules, a member who leaves cannot sell his or her apartment for profit to another private individual, but must sell it back to the co-op. And although some cooperators may bequeath their apartments to sons and daughters, there are relatively strict rules requiring relatives to be in residence for two years before the original tenant vacates. There is a ten-year–plus waiting list for these apartments.

The housing co-ops sponsored by the garment workers' unions were emulated in New York by the electrical and hospital workers' unions. Electchester, a Queens housing co-op, still exists. Local 1199 of the Service Employees International Union (SEIU) sponsored a co-op in Harlem near the East River, but sold it shortly after its construction. In other cities, few unions have followed the New York example. Instead, after World War II, the labor movement left solutions to the dire housing shortage to private real estate developers. In 1949, Congress failed to pass legislation on multidwelling public housing designed for low- and middle-income people, and instead supported a Federal Housing Administration low-interest loan program for certain categories of private home buyers—first veterans, and then middle-income people. The resulting one- and two-family housing boom temporarily satisfied the growing need for adequate shelter while spurring the growth of the appliance and construction industries, but the ultimate social costs were steep: Since the program was directed chiefly toward buyers of single-household dwellings, there was little use for it in most cities of the Northeast, and housing subdivisions began sprouting like weeds, many of them on former farmland. The mass suburbanization of the country had begun.

Farmers gladly sold all or some of their acreage to developers because they received a price greater than the land was worth for agriculture. Single-household homes soon occupied vast tracts of countryside. But although these subdivisions offered more comfort than city apartments, suburban sprawl changed social and cultural life. Each household needed one or two automobiles to perform nearly all tasks: food shopping, commuting to work, visiting friends and relatives, going to the movies and other entertainments. And the very concept of neighborhood was radically altered. Adults could no longer walk across the hall to borrow a cup of sugar; in some areas, kids stopped playing together in the streets—either there were not enough children to start a game of baseball or tag or Simon Says, or they lived too far apart. Parents had to drive their children to a playground, a ball field, or a friend's house.

My parents and their families were innate urban villagers. That most of their children—my cousins—became suburbanites reflects two major shifts in the culture. First, home ownership became the only way most people could enjoy a dwelling space congruent with the popular perception of the good life. Second, the shortage of decent urban housing drove many people to the suburbs who still preferred the cities for their plays, concerts and walking space. The suburbs, for all their comfort, are ecological disasters. They have eliminated land that could be used to grow food. They have cluttered the country with cars and trucks. Equally egregious, they have redefined social life in ways that produce isolation and alienation, not least because they cut people off from most forms of shared culture except for sports and television—one reason for the current reverse migration of many young people and also older people to the cities.

What Is to Be Done, Now?

The final question to confront in this discussion of the good life is whether we have reached a historical moment when capitalism is no longer a viable framework for popular aspirations. Put another way, is the crisis that matured in 2006–07 different from its historical antecedents? At this writing, we are in the eighth year of economic stagnation and decline, and it is more than four decades since Medicare and Medicaid, the last extensions of the social wage, were enacted. The Affordable Care Act, popularly known as Obamacare, is not an extension of the social wage, and it is an indication of what can and cannot be accomplished toward the good life within the capitalism framework today.

Obamacare, however the right may decry its supposed socialist tendencies, largely benefits the insurance industry. Although subscribers unable to afford health insurance do receive subsidies from the Federal government, they are still liable for copayments and left vulnerable by incomplete coverage. Since there is no provision in the legislation passed by Congress in 2010 for controlling health-care costs, we can expect reduced benefits over time for subscribers, which means that beneficiaries are likely to pay more out of their own pockets. It is also worth noting that the plans being offered come in different and unequal versions, according to how high a premium a subscriber, with or without a subsidy, can afford to pay. For example, the administration required insurance companies to offer mental health benefits, and they have, in four tiers. The Bronze tier has the lowest premium, but it requires the subscriber to contribute 40 percent of the cost of mental health treatments; the Platinum tier requires only a 10 percent copayment, but the monthly premiums are much more expensive.[11]

The only health care program that people of all income levels would be able to afford and that would guarantee equal basic coverage and level of care for all is the single-payer system. So the larger question about health care is whether single-payer, or socialized medicine, is likely to be achieved without a profound transformation in the current structure of political power. Considering the hostility of most of those who benefit from that structure toward all forms of socialism, it seems unlikely.

Nor is it likely that the high level of joblessness can be substantially reduced, which means we may be in the early stages of permanent mass unemployment in the United States, Western Europe, and developing countries. As I have argued here and elsewhere, even with a sharply reduced workday, guaranteed income, and jobs programs, the historically rapid pace of technological change will leave a substantial fraction of the population economically redundant even if the economy recovers to its early 2000s level. Of course, this evaluation does not vitiate the need for these adaptive reforms. Nor is it futile for a revived labor movement to intervene, globally, in the shape and intensity of technological innovation. But if we are on the cusp of an entirely new economic situation, then an entirely new set of political and economic arrangements is not only desirable, it is necessary.[12]

Capital will fight with every weapon at its command to hold on to power and wealth. Some individuals and groups with a big stake in the system might entertain proposals for cosmetic and incremental improvements, but they will resist compromising on serious redistributive measures and never agree to a genuine transfer of power. The stakes are too high, and now that they can no longer count on cyclical tendencies to come to the rescue of the market, they might opt for war as a solution, an alternative that has proven effective throughout the recent past and in the present. Yet war mobilization will not create the number of jobs it once did. Like industrial production, the production of war materiel is driven by new technologies and combat itself is no longer labor-intensive. Human soldiers have not disappeared, but their numbers have been reduced as drones and other computer-driven weapons take center stage.

The old alternative stares us starkly in the face: socialism or barbarism. For, as we are increasingly made aware, the real targets of modern war, including the so-called war on terror, are not enemy combatants but civilian populations. For the United States government and its NATO allies, techno-wars are won when "collateral" damage persuades the people to surrender their dream of autonomy and the elite to open their energy and mineral resources to Western capital.

Since the collapse of the Soviet Union and China's recent journey into a regulated mixed economy in which private ownership and investment are dominant, the term *socialism* has fallen on hard times. We have learned that neither capitalism nor the twentieth-century versions of socialism can be termed democracy if democracy is defined as popular control over the workplace, communities, and public life. Even authoritarian regimes are content to permit universal suffrage and allow voters to select candidates from competing political parties that promise to rule, if elected, within the existing setup. In the West and parts of Latin America, some speech and press freedoms are tolerated, although occasionally dissenters are jailed, publications banned, and individuals assassinated or driven into exile. Now almost a quarter century since the Soviet Union's demise distancing themselves from the legacy of actual dictatorial socialisms, some philosophers have proposed a new communist project. Given the history of communism, this medicine will seem too strong to most American workers and intellectuals, although in Europe and Latin America it has enjoyed some favor.

Looking beyond familiar labels, let us discuss concrete alternative visions for the good life. If you are a wage or salary worker you know that neither collective bargaining nor legislation has been able to maintain living standards, let alone improve them. Promises of career opportunities for those with postsecondary degrees have proven unreliable. In February 2013, the *New York Times* reported that the BA now carries the same weight as the high school diploma of yesteryear; for example, law firms in Atlanta now require a BA for entry-level clerical jobs.[13] Yet millions who start college drop out before obtaining their degrees, and many have only high school diplomas or even less at a time when some colleges are reducing enrollments, even as the demand for berths explodes. Formal credentials are no longer the ticket to a bright future.

An alternative path to that future would challenge the permanence of big private capital, beginning with the huge financial engines that control most of our economic, political, and social institutions. We could start by socializing the giant banks. I use the term *socializing* rather than *nationalizing* because a genuine alternative would be based on participatory, democratic governance by bank employees; small depositors, individuals as well as institutions such as nonprofit community organizations; and small businesses. Similarly, since large-scale industrial, insurance, and service corporations are publicly traded and often rely on government subsidies to sustain themselves, these, too, should be subject to the participatory, democratic governance of workers and consumers. Health and educational institutions should be similarly managed. Teachers, health care workers, students, parents, and residents would share control and decision making in their institutions. A society based on democratic participatory control was called a cooperative commonwealth by nineteenth-century socialists and anarchists and their prescriptions for building one were concrete, not abstract. Their descriptions of how production and services would be organized imply a massive transfer of power from private interests to the producers and their communities. Workers' and consumers' cooperatives producing goods and services would initially compete with supermarket chains and other private enterprises and eventually replace them.

To establish similarly self-managed health and educational institutions, workers and other community members would need to possess enough knowledge to make informed decisions. Universal specialized knowledge would not be necessary, but in health institutions, for example, the collective would have to understand such matters as consent in treatment regimes and what regimes might be subject to controversy, and be equipped to reach conclusions about a broad range of policy alternatives. In schools, in order to intervene in decisions regarding curriculum, pedagogical methods, and the use of technologies, for example, parents and teachers would need to study educational issues and be able to make informed choices when presented with alternative perspectives.

On the highest level of abstraction, self-managers would need to have a more or less clear conception of what good health care and education consist of. This requires hard work, but it is necessary if the constituents of these institutions are to have real decision-making powers. Above all, participants would need to understand the limits of these institutions. For instance, can we posit that the main determinant of health is the physician and the health care institutions, or are there other determinants, such as nutrition, water and air quality, and conditions of labor? Recognizing the links between the institutional framework and the larger environment would also be part of decision making.

We need not wait for radical social transformation of the prevailing system to begin implementing the vision of the cooperative commonwealth. We can set up democratic workers' co-ops by occupying factories and other facilities or by buying abandoned industrial and service spaces. Co-op housing, already part of the existing landscape, could be expanded to address workers' dwelling requirements, especially important in an era when most can no longer afford to buy single-family houses.

Urban-agricultural food partnerships are already functioning in New York and other states. Farmers bring their wares to markets set up in public spaces, quite often public parks. In some areas individual households can also subscribe to a farm distributor that delivers a full range of vegetables, meats and spices. These operations could be expanded, introduced into residential neighborhoods and sites adjacent to workplaces, especially if food co-ops took hold.

Of course, institutions that adopted popular forms of power in a country and world still framed by capitalism would remain subject to market fluctuations, technological challenges, and state repression—the latter especially if the cooperative commonwealth became a political ideology as well as a set of institutional practices. Any gains the movement made would have to be fiercely defended against laws stacked in favor of productive enterprises based on private property. For example, disused factories and offices occupied by workers would likely be reclaimed by the owners who abandoned them, as happened in Argentina, and the courts would more than likely sustain those claims even if the buildings had lain long empty and the owners had no further plans for them. Defending occupied spaces would become a major political fight, requiring mass, direct action.

A self-managed enterprise would face other challenges. It would have to realize a surplus over cost, and members would have to decide how to allocate it: to increased pay and benefits, equipment replacement, or projects of modernization and expansion. They would have to decide whether to keep the all of the surplus within the enterprise or share it with less successful comrades organizing other enterprises. They would have to agree on what should be produced, what labor processes, including technologies, should be used to produce it, and how to distribute it. They would have to be prepared to resolve these and also unexpected conflicts arising from specific situations.

Certainly, a major issue is how to raise start-up capital. Banks in Greece have refused to lend to co-ops, and there is no reason to believe that most banks in the United States would extend lines of credit to worker- managed enterprises, especially those begun as occupations in workspaces abandoned but still owned by other companies. Union pension funds might be made available; the only labor bank in New York, the Amalgamated Bank, might agree to lend to workers' co-ops. In any case, a co-op would almost surely be required to wage a fundraising campaign. In addition, most of them would require support from communities, sympathetic local unions, and socially committed professionals such as engineers, industrial planners, and accountants.

Another question is the role of unions. Even in an enterprise self-managed by workers, conflicts between the collective and an individual worker or shop department are possible, and in cases where peaceful resolution fails, so are strikes. Facing an impasse with a managing committee or with the whole collective, groups of workers might decide to take their grievances to the streets. Therefore the co-operative movement would need a fairly rigorous process for addressing differences, including those that cannot be settled by direct negotiation. Should workers' organizations be independent of the co-op? What happens when you create company unions like those representing workers in union offices? In any case, clearly workers will need a union even in a self-managed setup, and their union will have to participate in the management.

The Worker and the State

Since the early months of the Great Depression, for more than eighty-five years, workers' movements in the most industrially developed societies have addressed their protests and appeals to the state. In the United States, at first, it seemed impossible that the government, which for ten years had shown itself indifferent to workers' issues, would respond to the demands of those the economic crisis had left hungry and homeless. In 1930, national unemployment protests led by the left were quelled by police violence, and in 1932, the Hoover administration met the legendary Veterans Bonus March with military repression. Army Chief of Staff General Douglas MacArthur and his second-in-command, Major George S. Patton, were ordered to break up the march by force, and they did, using infantry, cavalry, and six tanks.

Some state and local governments provided "relief" by running soup kitchens and permitting the homeless to camp in city parks. The unemployed had little reason to believe that the national administration would respond with anything more than such inadequate palliatives. For them, as for most militants in the unions, the state was a collection of coercive apparatuses and institutions: the police, the courts, the prisons. Even the brief period of social reform in the decade before World War I had not changed their perception that like the capitalists, the state was their enemy. Nevertheless, they fought for the right to organize and assemble, for free speech in public spaces, and for legislative remedies for safety violations in factories. They hardly hoped that state institutions, including elected legislatures, would provide serious support for the unemployed, the aged, children, and the disabled.

They had few illusions. The unions themselves, many of which had been decimated in the 1920s, were mostly indifferent to the plight of the unemployed, although under pressure from militants the AFL established a committee to seek legislation for unemployment compensation.

But the committee was made up largely of left-wing trade unionists and did not have the backing of the largest and most powerful affiliates among the skilled trades. Outside the AFL, the small but active independent unions cooperated with the unemployed movement, targeting mostly local governments and the large financial and industrial corporations, which they believed were largely responsible for the mass suffering. They had little faith that politicians would act to alleviate that suffering, yet they made the state an arena because there were few alternatives.

Moreover, in 1932 organizers could see that the political situation was about to change. And indeed, the Roosevelt administration moved quickly to supply food and shelter to the urban and rural destitute and started a jobs program, though as we have seen this was not broadly based or large enough to significantly close the gap between wage labor and the third of the nation who were unemployed. Yet even many employed workers had short-time schedules that barely enabled them to survive. Official figures reckoned the jobless rate at 25 percent, but if we add in the regular hours not worked by short-time employees, the real figure grows by at least a third. In some parts of the country, whole communities were out of paid work.

The situation hit older workers hardest. The New Deal targeted its jobs programs to younger people. The WPA, government contracts to private companies, and the Civilian Conservation Corps created five million jobs in construction, urban cleanup, forestry, and services to rural areas such as health care and schooling.

Yet these programs and the New Deal legislation that followed represent the state's finest hour of intervention on behalf of the working class. In our current depression, what can workers realistically expect of today's politicians and what are they going to have to do for themselves?

If Not the State, Who?

From what sources other than government can we expect a new vision of the good life? In the past, when the working class and the sinking middle class struggled to keep their heads above water and see a better shore, they often turned to intellectuals for guidance. Radical scholars were not the only source of the radical imagination, but they were learned, did their research, and wrote well. In the nineteenth century Karl Marx was deeply involved in workers' movements, although he was hardly working-class. Pierre-Joseph Proudhon grew up in a working-class family and was quite poor, but even after he achieved a middle-class and political career he directed his scholarship and energies toward helping workers in their struggle for a better life— and world. Both of these men understood that the best chance for a free and just society lay in the working class, both because it produced society's wealth and because it was the first oppressed class in history to possess the capacity for self-organization.

Marx and Proudhon were classically trained intellectuals, educated in the traditions of civilization: philosophy, literature, history, science. Each in his own way concluded that freedom for the immense majority could not be achieved under capitalism and that the producers of the Industrial Age needed to take control of their own labor: of what is produced, how it is produced, and how it is disposed of. They were suspicious of solutions to workers' problems that depended on the capitalist state or on the leaders of bureaucratic organizations. They directed their prolific writings at working-class audiences. Marx popularized some of the key concepts of his masterwork *Capital* in pamphlets and wrote numerous articles for the workers' press.

In the United States, progressive unions once employed and consulted with labor intellectuals, who were the bearers of emancipatory ideas from Europe, mostly of a socialist, communist or anarchist nature. Some of the earliest labor intellectuals were refugees from the failed 1848 revolutions, principally those in Italy and Germany. Some, like socialists Daniel De Leon, Louis Boudin and Morris Hillquit, were professors or lawyers. In the first decades of the twentieth century, the labor and socialist presses flourished. The socialist pro-labor paper *Appeal to Reason* had a circulation of 700,000 in 1912; *The Masses*, a radical cultural magazine sympathetic to the Industrial Workers of the World (IWW) circulated in the arts communities but also mobilized intellectuals and artists to support strikes. The journalist John Reed organized an astoundingly successful Madison Square Garden pageant complete with dance, music, and poetry to support the Paterson, New

Jersey silk workers' strike. He also organized New York families to take in strikers' children for the duration of the action, an innovative tactic conceived during the famous Bread and Roses textile strike in Lawrence, Massachusetts, which was largely led by women workers and was the first to use a moving picket line. Intellectuals joined their voices to the workers' in Lawrence as well.

In the 1930s, the fledgling industrial labor movement and some of the AFL affiliates sponsored or supported labor schools. A. J. Muste, a Protestant minister, began his labor career right after World War I by organizing the Amalgamated Textile Workers union, which mounted some important strikes in the 1920s. When the ATW was severely disabled by a fierce antiunion employer offensive, Muste, with initial AFL support, founded Brookwood Labor College to educate both rank-and-file workers and organizers in Western culture and create a new generation of labor intellectuals within the union movement.[14] Dissatisfied with the left-wing parties—the Socialists were too mild and the Communists were too subservient to Moscow—in 1930 he spearheaded the formation of the American Workers Party, which played an important role in organizing the unemployed and was crucial to the success of the Auto-Lite strike in Toledo, Ohio, and other labor struggles, chiefly in the Midwest. The new party attracted some of the leading radical intellectuals of the moment, among them Sidney Hook, whose books were arguably the most original contributions to Marxism by any American before World War II. The communists and socialists were prime sources of new ideas, were labor's teachers and writers, and without them labor education and research would not have been possible.

Left-wing unions worked with other radicals in sponsoring health care insurance for workers long before Medicare and union contracts were able to provide it. These unions also ran schools that offered broad education to their members and summer camps for their kids. The Ladies' Garment Workers and the Auto Workers maintained resorts where workers and their families could vacation. The resorts provided recreational facilities but also offered lectures, films, and other cultural events. The Socialists sponsored the Arbeiter Ring, or Workmen's Circle, which was founded by radical Jewish labor groups, and the Communists organized a parallel institution, the International Workers Order, which was more diverse, with Jewish, Hungarian, Finnish, Italian, and other "federations" in many major cities.[15] Both organizations offered life insurance, medical services—including dental care—and cultural activities. The IWO fell victim to the Cold War, as did many CP-sponsored institutions. The Workmen's Circle still exists, but although it retains a politically progressive mission statement, it has largely become a Jewish cultural organization, with branches in New York, Boston, and Los Angeles.

As the welfare state slowly disintegrates, we might ask whether some of these institutions should be reestablished on terms that can meet modern workers' needs. Should a new labor movement offer a series of community services to a new generation of workers, inside and outside the unions, including a cultural and political education that would breed a fresh generation of radical intellectuals equipped to address economic, social, and political conditions today?

When Walter Reuther, the former Socialist, became president of the UAW after World War II, he convened a kitchen cabinet of educators, journalists, and staff functionaries who were invariably to his left and infused the leadership with ideas that went beyond ordinary trade union business. Among them was the idea that the union should intervene in issues of corporate management such as price policy, and that workers should demand the right to regulate the pace of their labor. Early in his tenure Reuther liked to repeat the slogan of the Amalgamated Clothing Workers: "Labor Will Rule." Many in his informal cabinet were socialists and ex-Trotskyists, and one, Brendan Sexton, had been a leader of the New York Workers Alliance, a movement for the unemployed jointly organized by the Socialist and Communist parties in the mid-1930s.

The officers of the Clothing Workers and Garment Workers also employed intellectuals, among them the former Communist and left-wing socialist J. B. S. Hardman, and Gus Tyler, a former leader of the revolutionary caucus in the Socialist Party. Many newly organized industrial unions called upon intellectuals to conduct education programs that went beyond contract and grievance training. Highlander Folk School in Monteagle, Tennessee, which later conducted educational programs for civil rights activists, began as a labor school, concentrating its work on assisting Southern organizers. Highlander and its director, Myles Horton, were subjected to fierce red-baiting during the Cold War, but in the 1960s their legacy was a beacon for the insurgent black freedom movement. Participants included Rosa Parks and many members of the Student Nonviolent Coordinating Committee (SNCC). Martin Luther King was an intellectual leader, and so was Bayard Rustin, the principal organizer of the 1963 March on Washington.

Some unions still hire intellectuals as functionaries of their political machine. They edit the newspaper, do administrative work, and sometimes serve as organizing and line staff. But since unions have renounced a transformative vision of social and political relations, they no longer see the necessity of working with intellectuals who can help prepare the members and workers generally for participating in the work of social transformation.

Of course, professional intellectuals are not labor's only possible source of ideas—there have always been intellectuals among factory, office, retail, and service workers. But professional intellectuals are needed to help create a collective intellect, so that vigorous new thinkers arise from the rank and file to replace them. Professional intellectuals need not be the only formulators of a new vision of the good life, but they may be needed to boldly put the questions associated with the good life back on the table. As we have seen, even political groups motivated by the promise of new social arrangements refrain from openly discussing their transformative views in their trade unions or in public forums, for fear they will be labeled as sectarians and lose access to the rank and file.

This self-censorship among U.S. radicals is nothing new. It dates from two closely related developments: Samuel Gompers's refusal to link the labor movement to an ideological flag, a stance that led more radical thinkers to form the rival IWW; and the Socialist Party's entry, with both feet, into the electoral arena, where the terms of engagement implied acceptance of the capitalist system as the given framework within which the struggles for social reform were to be conducted. Even the Communists followed this playbook after 1934. The CP became the virtual left wing of the Democratic Party during the Roosevelt administration and a major force in militant unionism that, however, carefully avoided introducing radical ideas into its trade union policies. The furthest boundary of its radicalism was simply antifascism. And the repressive McCarthyist era of the 1950s and early 1960s struck a fear into the left from which it has never recovered.

The New Left of the 1960s did articulate the idea of "participatory democracy," which proposed that democracy was not merely the opportunity to vote for traditional political parties: it was a system in which ordinary people directly made the decisions that affected their lives. This concept closely expressed the CIO program of workplace and union democracy, which had mostly disappeared in the postwar era. This form of democracy was an objective of the community organizing of the Students for a Democratic Society (SDS), but in the late 1960s this focus was partly lost, overwhelmed by the pressures of the antiwar and civil rights struggles. It is worth noting that many of the organizers of the postwar movements for union reform had cut their teeth on the doctrine of participatory democracy and later spiked it with a heavy dose of Marxism. They carried the ideas of the New Left into the unions, but largely in a syndical form. Socialist and Communist schools continued to offer a radical education, mostly of the Marxist variety, until the 1950s. But on the ground, in their trade union and other popular activities, the radicals confined their interventions to immediate issues.

Today, labor education has suffered sharp decline. After World War II, some unions relied primarily on university-based union leadership programs to train their shop-level stewards and officers in contract administration, labor law, and political action; others sent their full-time organizing and service staff to short-term education and training sessions offered by the universities. In the 1970s, worker education entered a new phase when some universities began offering degree programs to union members and their families. There is intellectual training available through the unions today. But it is not radical intellectual training. What has disappeared is the radical imagination.

CHAPTER SEVEN
Toward a New Labor Movement, Part Two

Urgent Tasks of a New Labor Movement

Marx famously said that the movement cannot draw its inspiration from the past. The point is still valid, yet there are some historical lessons and models crucial to consider as we shape a new vision for labor.

One of the most important is that the workers' movement must be broader and more inclusive than the unions. Typically, unions are organized and designed to deal with workplace issues, though they sometimes address problems in workers' everyday lives. When unions form coalitions with community groups to fight for better education, housing, and public transportation, or against the super-exploitation of the working poor, that shows a broader, grander conception of labor activism and suggests a basis for the new labor movement. Occupy Wall Street stemmed from the salaried middle class, workers still unfamiliar to and largely ignored by traditional unions, yet it was a workers' movement and it presented—may still present—an opportunity for exactly this kind of creative, transformative alliance.

Further: In order to build a new workers' movement, activists need their own organizations that are distinct from the unions and can work to make the unions more democratic and more combative in challenging capital and the repressive state, and these organizations cannot confine their efforts to caucus work. The old labor movement grew fastest and fought most boldly when most of its radicals were members of active organizations independent of the established unions: the IWW, which was a separate labor entity, the Socialist and Communist parties, and the anarchist federations. These groups gave them their political and ideological bearings.

In 1920, while the AFL oscillated between complacency and defeatism, militant activists, many of them Communists who had helped organize the IWW, founded the Trade Union Education League to intervene in workers' struggles. TUEL organized industrial unions, resisted employer attacks on workers' living standards and working conditions, and educated rank-and-file militants about the class struggle and the need for an alternative to capitalism.

Today, labor's radicals are either organized in relatively small ideological/political formations or else operate as individuals; in the main, these entities have little or nothing to do with one another. Those in the New York City transit system do not meet together between union elections, instead operating as distinct factions. The rank-and-file group Teamsters for a Democratic Union works within the Teamsters and does not reach out to other unions' militant groups, let alone form alliances with workers' centers, the Taxi Drivers, or radical nurses' and domestic workers' groups. A new radical workers' movement would have to cross organizational and ideological boundaries.

Small political groups have their own leaders and specific interests and orientations, and working together might be difficult and certainly messy. But unless the left is determined to remain fragmented, without a genuine social and political impact, it needs a national organization formed of these groups, outside as well as within the unions. The new organization might even be able to found new unions in sectors where established organizers have either failed or never tried—among the restaurant workers and day laborers, for example, and among the scientific, administrative, and technical formations.[1]

An effective strategy for this kind of organization is to form committees in and out of workplaces. These committees would not be traditional unions. They would not immediately ask people to sign union cards in preparation for an NLRB representational election. Instead, they would start as discussion or study groups focused on immediate problems in the workplace and outside. Certainly they might organize to make demands on their employers or join with community groups and unions in fighting for common goals. But they might also want to study labor theory, examine the history and current state of union and broader workers' movements in their own professions or occupations, and explore appropriate forms of organization for a new labor movement. These committees would be allied with one another, affiliated through the new TUEL or whatever name is affixed to the independent labor organization. Both the national organization and the committees would raise money through membership dues, avoiding the complications and restrictions of foundation grants and gifts from rich donors.

Another question to consider is whether a new labor movement should sponsor and organize minority unions. Minority unions petition or strike for recognition from individual employers. If successful, they represent only workers who have joined the union. Some established unions may eventually opt to form minority unions, but there is little current movement in this direction; most are fixated on majority representation.

Any association that chooses to independently organize workers within an established union's jurisdiction, even workers from a group that the union has effectively abandoned, is going to be seen as a threat.[2] This is not necessarily a bad thing: competition may goad the conventional unions to undertake their own organizing. As we have seen, competitive unionism is often a stimulus to mobilization and ultimate success. The new labor movement should welcome the entry of the old unions into the fray; one of the historical functions of left-led unions has been to awaken the slumbering mainstream.

What About the Unions?

Collective bargaining, the mainstream union solution, has fallen on hard times. The contract, once a compromise between workers and capital in the private sector and between public workers and the state, is a compromise no longer. Today, more often than not, it is a union's signed surrender. There is a place for bargaining; it will remain an important part of the arsenal of labor action, but the old formulas for it no longer work. It is time to move on. Here, then, are my ten theses, or ten-point manifesto, for a new labor movement, modestly offered:

1. Bargaining over wages, working conditions, and benefits need not culminate in a contract. If the workers' collective power is sufficient to avoid a formal agreement, they are better off without one. If they must sign one, it should not include a no-strike provision. And if the workers are not strong enough to impose a deal that does not prohibit strikes during the life of the agreement, then the life of the agreement should be short—say, one year—and the terms should specify exceptional conditions in which workers may withhold their labor, such as discriminatory discharge or an arbitrary change in the work process.

2. The fight for shorter hours is essential and should be waged as a prolonged two-pronged attack: a strong push for legislation that mandates a reduced workday and workweek and direct action in the form of marches, mass demonstrations, and strike activity. This battle must be fought by the new and old labor movements.[3]

3. There must be a national campaign to enact a guaranteed income equal to the minimum wage and/or unemployment compensation, whichever is higher. The guaranteed wage should take regional conditions such as housing, transportation, and food prices into account.

4. More than 800 local unions have endorsed single-payer health care, and single-payer legislation has been introduced in Congress. The national unions and liberal center, instead of joining the fight to enact it, backed the Affordable Care Act, the Obama administration's gift to the insurance companies. The fight for socialized medicine is not over, but it won't succeed until and unless a new labor movement and a large fraction of the old one take up the cudgel together. This ought to be a priority of radicals who hope to revive the labor movement.

5. Deindustrialization and deterioration of the food sold in supermarkets have given workers a clear reason to ally with community activist groups and start their own producer and consumer co-ops, which would provide not only higher-quality food but also good jobs. Instead of relying on institutions of finance capital, workers

need to create credit unions dedicated, in part, to financing these ventures, determining the best approach by a thorough study of federal and state credit union regulations.

6. The rank and file should demand the right to create minority unions. If traditional unions refuse, the radical labor movement should seize the opportunity to replace the old order altogether.

7. The fight against racial, gender, and ethnic discrimination in hiring, especially in the skilled trades, has languished for too long. One of the most egregious illusions today is that all remaining decent jobs require post-secondary credentials; this is far from true. Many good semi-skilled factory jobs have disappeared, but there are actual shortages of several kinds of craft labor—tool and die makers, ironworkers, and wheelwrights, among others. There are jobs in these trades, but not for all comers; they remain largely the property of white males. In the 1960s and 1970s, when independent black workers' organizations fought through direct action and lawsuits for jobs in the skilled construction and goods production trades, there were some breakthroughs, as the craft unions sought to accommodate these movements. But the demonstrations, work-site disruptions, and legal challenges came to an end, and few further gains were made. It is time to resume the struggle.

8. Both new unions and old should demand and provoke organization of the vast and growing population of precarious workers, whether such unions are recognized by employers or not. If most of the old unions continue to slumber on this issue, new ones must rise and step in. Traditional labor leaders will scream bloody murder, or at least "Dual unionism!"—but if history is any guide, once the radicals take independent action, we can expect the establishment to jump in too. Then the fun begins.[4]

9. The long-standing struggle for union democracy must go on. But the rank-and-file caucuses need not assume union leadership under the present crumbling labor law. Both the original law and its Taft-Hartley amendment must be challenged. They are the key reason why the rank-and-file demand for "a decent contract" is antediluvian. Rank-and-file caucuses must direct their efforts to building alliances with the 247 existing workers' centers and

organizations, such as the Taxi Workers Alliances, Domestic Workers United and the National Domestic Workers Alliance, Our Walmart, the Restaurant Opportunities Center in New York. These are movements without contracts, yet they often take direct action and bargain with the state and private employers over their demands, and such organizations may be the right template for a new labor movement.

10. Many unions speak of the urgent need for a truly global labor movement. But even as Chinese, Indian, Bangladeshi, and Greek workers engage in mass strikes and job actions, and Mexican minority unions struggle for decent wages and working conditions, mainstream U.S. labor continues to sit on the sidelines. Only the small but spunky United Electrical Workers, the Steelworkers, and the Communications Workers of America have reached beyond our borders to assist these battles, and their efforts, except for UEW's, are sporadic. One of the major tasks of the new labor movement will be overcoming the implicit and explicit nationalism that afflicts workers and their unions. A globally divided workers' movement inevitably sinks into racism. Recall the loud labor-union cries against the Yellow Peril, not only in the nineteenth century but in the twentieth century as well. Lately, China has been largely exempt from such reaction because of the close ties between American business and Chinese entrepreneurs and their government sponsors. When these ties begin to unravel under pressure from insurgent Chinese workers' movements, the Yellow Peril fantasy will rear its ugly head again, unless steps are taken now to cement relations between U.S. labor and the Chinese and Indian insurgencies.

The Labor Movement and Climate Change

Only the loony-tunes wings of politics and religion deny the reality of climate change and the urgent need to address it. Sadly, that's a pretty big swath, including significant sections of the Republican Party and religious fundamentalists who cannot accept any proposition that has not been sanctioned by the Bible—except, of course, the propositions of capitalism regarding the sanctity of private property and hard work.

The unions are aware of and rhetorically support the modest efforts of the Obama administration to deal with global warming by reducing carbon emissions. But when the chips are down, that is, when jobs may be on the line, the AFL-CIO supports environmentally damaging projects such as the Keystone Pipeline. This regressive stance is not surprising given that the economic depression, which has fallen hard on construction workers and the AFL-CIO Construction Trades Department is the backbone of traditional unionism. But if it is understandable it is also regrettable and short-sighted: the construction jobs offered by the pipeline, even if they go to union labor, will be relatively short-lived, and the number of maintenance jobs that remain will not be significant. The social and environmental costs of the pipeline's construction and operation, however, will be long-term and far outweigh the benefits. Water quality is likely to be affected, and rich farmland from Nebraska to Florida impaired, perhaps for generations. But the unions see employment as their primary issue and rely on congressional findings that the project would pose no serious hazards, despite numerous studies that indicate otherwise.

Yet one of the crucial aspects of the environmental crisis is its long-term threat to jobs and to working-class quality of life. Global warming is causing floods, droughts, and sudden temperature changes that disturb ecosystems and disrupt crop production. It is in workers' best interests to fight for the environment rather than labor against it.

And workers are in a powerful position to do it, because they are the producers of all products and services, environmentally sound and otherwise. They could join the fight to replace fossil fuels such as oil and coal with renewable fuels, a process that would also provide jobs. Because fossil fuels are finite and will eventually disappear no matter what methods are found for their extraction, massive expansion of public transit is another positive solution labor should be actively pursuing. Workers should be in the vanguard of consumer change, helping to eliminate products associated with human illness and environmental damage. For every job lost in the retirement of a deleterious good or service, one can be created to produce a better one.

Finally, workers need to press for a moratorium on the spread of suburbs, which are ecologically unsustainable because of their contribution to excessive consumption and also tie up valuable farmland and drain water supplies. All of these shifts in political perception and economic priorities would severely reduce large sectors of our industrial base, and with them, jobs. But new jobs would be created, in the renewable fuels industry, in increased agriculture and food processing, in reconstruction and maintenance of infrastructure, and a greatly expanded public service sector.

And of course a workers' movement determined to save the planet from wanton consumer capitalism would necessarily demand shorter hours, guaranteed income, and a redefinition of the relationship of work to life.

The Intellectual Mission

Clearly there are good reasons for labor to take the long-term, broader global view of its purpose and of the purpose of work itself. This new labor movement would have to liberate itself from parochialism, launching a major program to educate workers on the stakes involved as they decide whether or not to act decisively to avert the coming calamity. Forgetting their own desperate economic need to be saved and instead joining the saviors of the planet will take a strong revival of the radical imagination.

And so worker education would be one of the primary tasks of a new labor movement. The curriculum would include but also go far beyond issues of collective bargaining, labor history, and the like. Questions of culture, social and political theory, philosophy, social and political history would be its equally necessary components.

As their perspectives broadened, eventually the small groups of radical democratic leftists would see the importance of working together in an ideologically diverse revolutionary political formation. This formation would differ from those formed during the past century and a half. In the first place, it would include anarchists, socialists, and communists, open to discussing with one another the basic questions of a future society: how to address the medium-term issue of structural reforms or, better, nonreformist reforms like shorter hours and guaranteed income;[5] how to provide for universal social wage such as retirement, health care and jobless benefits. The new political formation will require a theory of the state. It is not enough to call for tearing down the present government root and branch. Even after the current opponents of a universal good life have been neutralized or defeated, another form of repressive state could arise. But there would have to be some kind of administration, under workers' and popular self-management, capable of providing for a wide range of public goods and services without possessing repressive authority. Who will maintain bridges, roads, and airports, under what organizational tent? Who will maintain communications systems such as the telephone, the Internet, and social media? Who will implement and administer programs for young children, the retired, and the disabled? Would the political formation support and help organize workers' and consumer cooperatives, or be based on them?

Other questions remain. There is the issue of scientific and technical innovation. To save jobs, are we content to revert to a pretechnological age? If not, whatever system we put in place of our current state would have to regulate the introduction of new technology and provide for changes it created in the job situation. And, of course, how will we finally address the ecological and climate crisis without institutions of coordination?[6] The political formation must initiate a series of discussions on the issue, but, in contrast to the mainstream environmental movement, it would give high priority to the economic consequences of a thorough program of energy transformation from fossil to sustainable fuels and the drastic reduction of carbon emissions, which would starkly affect chemical production and the entire basis of consumer society. The debate would have to address problems of agriculture; specifically, the reinstitution of small, organic farms and the breakup of the food oligopolies. Finally, it would have to craft a radical approach to technological innovation in the workplace and in the society at large.

Real change, beyond questions of who owns the means of material and mental production, entails a new course of everyday life. The transition from consumerism to another conception of free time would be a long and difficult process. It would take new conceptions of time and space, where public life is no longer dictated from above; the built environment would be redesigned to encourage conviviality. We have all become habituated to ways of life that reinforce the prevailing setup. A commitment to the transformation of the everyday would distinguish this political formation from most of its predecessors, which saw the relationship of large-scale productive-property ownership and state power as the final framework of social transformation. Changing the life of the human race entails more than the program of early-twentieth-century revolutions ever envisioned. It means changing fundamental personal and social relations as well as the relationships involved in economic production.

What should we call the political formation that can dream, and do, all of this? Socialist, communist, cooperative commonwealth? Or some name entirely new? Despite past efforts, during different moments of revolutionary upheaval, to form workers' councils under the banner of socialism or communism, the legacy of both of these historical movements is statist. The Socialists tended to interpret socialism as an expanded social welfare state, its modestly redistributive measures taken within, not against, capitalist social relations. The Communists emulated the Soviet model and were throughout their heyday loyal to the regime, and so lost any conception of workers self-management. The anti-Communist left focused on anti-imperialist struggles and shop-floor democracy, particularly rank-and-file unionism, but did not challenge, in their practice, the underlying basis of labor relations. For these reasons we do need a different term to describe the ideology and formation that will achieve the good life. The virtue of *cooperative commonwealth* is its descriptive as well as prescriptive character. It signals what a self-managed society would look like: antibureaucratic, anticapitalist, truly democratic.

We have entered a moment in history when the alternative to direct action seems starker than ever: Capitalism promises nothing and delivers misery for a large chunk of the populations of the planet. The global masters of the system seem to disregard all movements; even European general strikes are shrugged off as long as combatants refuse to up the ante of their protests. The only way to challenge this repressive system is to take to the streets and occupy—and run—the key workplaces. This is a tall order, and will have to be filled step by step.

Much of this book has explored those steps and the issues surrounding them. To recap:

First, we have to form a militant minority within the unions and larger workers' movement. Second, we need to address intransigent situations with innovative direct action, as the labor movement did with the Walmart and fast-food walkouts. These actions were taken without union recognition or expectations of a contract, and can and should be reproduced on a wider scale. Third, the militant minority can create educational programs to help create workers' organic intellectuals. Fourth, labor activists should also fight for better housing, public schooling, and transportation. Occupy has led the way by resisting foreclosures. The question of a broader program of publicly financed housing at genuinely affordable rents should be addressed as well.

Finally, since state welfare functions have been all but shredded by both the legislative right and elements of the liberal center, the new labor movement may decide to take a leaf from the Black Panthers' urban arsenal and launch breakfast programs, street festivals, alternative schools for children and youth and adult "universities" that would offer literacy in a broad program of history, literature and visual arts, political economy and social theory. These initiatives would wrench labor's dependence away from an indifferent and increasingly repressive state.

The liberal mainstream may hang back on these issues, but the volatility of the current and future situation will force the militant minority to begin to act. If they lead, the majority will follow. It is time to begin the journey.

Endnotes

Preface

1 The Labor Relations Act retained the option of minority unionism, but this feature has largely been ignored by organized labor. However, as we shall see, there are a growing number of labor organizations that do not seek contracts or traditional collective bargaining rights.

2 Under NLRB provisions if a company recognizes and bargains with a minority union, only union members benefit from the agreement.

Introduction

1 Collective bargaining was not new. Unions in the apparel and mining industries had previously engaged in this practice. But the general rule was that workers' demands were won chiefly through strikes and other types of direct action.

2 Renamed Congress of Industrial Organizations (CIO) after they broke from the AFL.

3 Ira Kipnis, *The American Socialist Movement 1897–1912*, Chicago: Haymarket Books, 2004 [1952], 335–40.

4 Except in 1924 and 1972, when the AFL and its successor, AFL-CIO, respectively, refused to support the Democratic candidate.

5 Syndicalists hold that workers' organizations at the point of production are the carriers of the new society. They are generally hostile to representative

institutions, confining their political intervention to guaranteeing free speech and the right to organize.

6 Rutgers University Law Professor James Gray Pope has determined restricting the right to strike to be a First Amendment violation, but the courts have not so ruled on it.

7 For an expanded account of this, see Chapter 5.

8 Work-to-rule is the practice of doing exactly what is required by the workplace rules and no more, which can cause a production slowdown (for example, if workers refuse to do voluntary overtime).

9 See Howard Kimeldorf, *Battling for American Labor*, Berkeley and Los Angeles: University of California Press, 1999. Kimeldorf examines two unions of the early twentieth century, an AFL craft local and an IWW dockworkers' local. He finds that at the practical level they were similar. Both relied on direct action.

10 C. Wright Mills, *The New Men of Power: America's Labor Leaders*, New York: Oxford University Press, 2009 [1948], 224.

11 It is true that in late fall 2012 the Food and Commercial Workers and the Service Employees supported minority strikes against Walmart and a number of fast-food corporations. We shall discuss the significance of this departure later in the book. It remains a question whether these or other unions will mount sustained strike activities and organizing efforts in these sectors.

12 Exceptionally, in 1946 and 1947 UAW president Walter Reuther demanded that car companies "open the books" to show profit margins before raising prices. Swiftly rebuffed, Reuther became a fervent advocate of the permanent war economy as the best means to create new jobs.

13 C. Wright Mills, *White Collar*, New York: Oxford University Press, 2009 [1951].

1. The Winter of Our Discontent

1 Peter Rachleff, "Labor History for the Future," *Social Policy* Fall 2012.

2 For example, the courts have ratified employers' "free speech" rights to address workers during a Labor Board–supervised representation election. Although employers do not have the right to threaten to move a shop, fire workers, or reduce operations if the union wins, antiunion lawyers have

perfected language that effectively threatens workers with these consequences.

3 Henri Lefebvre, *The Explosion*, New York: Monthly Review Press, 1970.

4 During the anti–Vietnam War movement the Madison campus was a scene of perpetual protest. When the TAA invited me to meet with them in 1970, my public talk was interrupted so that the students could participate in the daily march from the center of the campus up a long hill to the Army-Math building, a trek that ended in a tear gas attack by the police. When we arrived back at the meeting hall, I resumed my speech.

5 Engels to J. Bloch, in *Karl Marx and Frederick Engels: Selected Correspondence*, Moscow: Foreign Languages Publishing House, 1956, p. 498.

6 Unless, of course, the car has been evaluated as a genuine classic: more than a quarter-century old and in mint condition.

7 Chapter 6 will discuss this issue more extensively.

8 These include the invitations to insider trading prevalent in the halls of Congress. Members are apprised of lucrative investment opportunities in advance of official market trades. Many of them emerge rich from these tips and they are mindful of their benefactors.

9 After Swope's passing, GE became one of the most antiunion large corporations, despite its extensive unionization.

2. *The Mass Psychology of Liberalism*

1 The river was finally partially restored, thanks mostly to the work of social movements whose condemnations and direct action forced the state to force the companies to take some responsibility for the cleanup.

2 Despite unswerving efforts at housecleaning by Reuther and Steelworker president Phillip Murray and his successor David Mcdonald, some large locals in those unions remained in the hands of the left or of coalitions in which the left played an important role. The most notable examples are the huge Ford Local 600 in River Rouge, Michigan; Local 1010 at Inland Steel, a strong rank-and-file movement in South Chicago steel mills; and New York's UAW Local 259. Even so, the legendary UAW vice-president for aircraft Wyndam Mortimer; organizer Bob Travis, who was among the key catalysts of the sit-down strikes at General Motors in Flint; and scores of CP union activists were deprived of their

union posts and sometimes their jobs as well. The UAW and the Steelworkers openly collaborated with FBI and other federal agents in these purges.

3 For a fuller discussion of the role of the New York Intellectuals in the anti-communist crusade, see Stanley Aronowitz, *Taking it Big: C.Wright Mills and the Making of Political Intellectuals*, New York: Columbia University Press, 2012.

4 Most other unions turned their backs on the strike because it was a wildcat action directed against the leadership of an AFL-CIO affiliate. Later, after he was successfully ousted by a rank-and-file movement, Tony Boyle, the Miners' president, went to jail.

3. The Rise and Fall of the Modern Labor Movement

1 The Wagner-Murray-Dingell Bill, which would have given the United States a system similar to the British Health Service, went down in flames under the powerful opposition of the American Medical Association. The term *supplementary* refers to the slow increases awarded to recipients of Social Security payments, which in an increasingly conservative political environment failed to keep pace with the cost of living. Part of the problem is that employer and worker contributions to the fund are capped. Removal of the cap would permit higher monthly benefits and make private pensions less crucial, especially in a time when many companies are reducing or eliminating them.

2 This is discussed in more detail in Chapter 4.

3 Barbara S. Griffith, *The Crisis of American Labor: Operation Dixie and the Defeat of the CIO,* Philadelphia: Temple University Press, 1988, and Steve Rosswurm, "Introduction: An Overview and Assessment of the CIO's Expelled Unions," *The CIO's Left Led Unions*, ed. Steve Rosswurm, New Brunswick, NJ: Rutgers University Press, 1992.

4 See Janet Irons, *Testing the New Deal*, Champaign Urbana: University of Illinois Press, 2000, for the history of the 1934 national textile strike.

5 David Macaray, "The Dreadful Caterpillar Strike," *Huffington Post.*

6 Victor Gotbaum, who trained to be a diplomat but became a professional union official, was the former executive director of AFSCME's District Council 37's 150,000 members, then left his office to became a consultant.

More recently, Andy Stern left the presidency of the giant Service Employees union but did not return to the public workplace. None of the successive presidents of the UAW after Walter Reuther's death in 1970 returned to auto factories or to local union offices.

4. The Struggle for Union Reform

1 "Jurisdictional wars" refer to the plethora of conflicts between unions claiming their right to organize in a specific industry or trade. These conflicts arose internally among AFL affiliates as well as CIO affiliates and continue to appear periodically within the AFL-CIO.

2 The precaution was hardly needed; the merger definitively ended the twenty-year era of competitive unionism that began with the split in labor's ranks between craft and industrial ideologies.

3 I owe this insight to Jonathan Cutler. See his study of UAW Ford Local 600, *Labor's Time: Shorter Hours, the UAW, and the Struggle for American Unionism*, Philadelphia: Temple University Press, 2004.

4 The incumbent was Jackie Presser, who was under federal indictment and forced to step down. The 1991 vote for his replacement was deeply significant: it was the first secret-ballot election in Teamster history.

5 *Barn* is the trucking industry's name for the garage where drivers pick up their vehicles at the beginning of the workday and return them at the end of the shift. The barn is also where workers congregate to share experiences, gripe about working conditions, and gossip.

6 Although the Teamsters were readmitted into the AFL-CIO after a period of expulsion, and could not longer raid established union jurisdictions, the no-raid pact with the Federation did not prevent affiliates to compete for unorganized workers.

7 This evaluation system was also pushed by the Obama administration, whose education secretary, Arne Duncan, had been Chicago's schools chancellor.

8 *Chicago Tribune*, Dec. 17, 2012.

9 Kim Moody's excellent description of labor's decline and his plea for rank-and-file union reform, *US Labor in Trouble and Transition*, is a case in point. His book is chiefly devoted to the globalization of industrial

production. Although he provides detailed accounts of the geography and demography of industrial production and of union reform, and addresses some of the new developments in the labor movement such as workers centers, he offers no sustained treatment of contingent and part-time labor and virtually ignores the fate of public employees unions, which had by the early 2000s had become the majority sector of U.S. unionism. He gives short shrift to the growth of professional and technical labor accompanying technological transformation and to the use of precarious labor that had already begun to dominate the retail and wholesale sectors. Similarly, he does not examine the nature of the labor process, either in industrial production or the service industries, or the effects of technological change on the size, composition and character of work. These omissions are serious because they reveal the limits of "workerism"—the ideology that privileges the industrial worker—and industrial unionism in the quest for a new labor movement. They also show the limits of institutional focus on class and labor.

5. The Underlying Failure of Organized Labor

1 In this context, "older" signifies workers over forty or forty-five, and certainly those over fifty.

2 For a description and analysis of FACET see Robert Heifetz "The Role of Professional and Technical Workers in Social Transformation," *Monthly Review* December 2000.

3 I recall Marvin Miller's talk to a regional Steelworkers' conference in the late 1950s. Then a staff economist for the union (who later won fame as the Moses of sports unionism when he freed Major League Baseball players from the reserve clause), Miller warned the assembly that while the U.S. steel industry resisted advanced technology, the reconstructed Japanese and European steel industries had adopted it, and he predicted significant foreign-steel imports and steep employment cuts in domestic steel. His speech was ignored then, but later vindicated by events.

4 I am not endorsing protectionism in general, but the unions needed protection in order to negotiate over technological changes, even those they would eventually have to accept. Their usual response to European and Japanese imports was to echo free market and nationalist appeals to "buy American."

5   For a fuller discussion of the consequences of the Guaranteed Annual Wage (GAW, the term for the East and Gulf Coast agreements) for Brooklyn's sprawling seaport, see William DiFazio, *Longshoremen: Community and Resistance on the Brooklyn Waterfront*, Bergin & Garvey, 1985. Contrary to the received wisdom that nonwork would lead to widespread alcoholism, anomie and psychological depression, DiFazio finds that being relieved of the daily grind of labor freed longshore workers to spend more time with their families, engage in creative activities such as crafts, and socialize with each other. In a personal conversation with me, fifty years later, he observed that many workers, including his father, extended their life expectancy by decades, compared to the mortality among longshore workers prior to the GAW.

6   For a further discussion of this expectation, see Stanley Aronowitz, *From the Ashes of the Old*, Boston: Houghton Mifflin, 1998.

7   Compare that to most industrially developed countries in the Eurozone. In France, jobless benefits at 80 percent of the last several years of employment are guaranteed for two years. Workers are able to return to school, tuition-free, to acquire new skills or trades. After two years, guaranteed income is available, but at a lower rate.

8   This calculation does not take into account the huge expansion in the retail and wholesale trades, which employ millions of workers, many of whom do not have full-time jobs. Restaurants are the chief employer of this precariat, but discount big-box department store chains like Walmart and Target have also added several million mostly part-time, hourly wage workers.

9   The California Nurses Association is an exception. It has sponsored a research institute that, responding to the Affordable Care Act's invocation to health providers to propose plans for patient-centered health care, has issued several reports that reflect its perspective on qualitative aspects. But the largest union of health care workers, SEIU 1199, which represents hundreds of thousands of members in the Northeast, Middle Atlantic States, and part of the Midwest, has not yet addressed autonomy issues.

10 Anemona Hartocollis, "New York Ties Doctors' Pay to Care Issues," *New York Times*, January 12, 2013.

11 Hence, universities shared with companies like IBM in the production of knowledge that led to the development of the personal computer in the 1980s.

12 One of the worst usual practices among credit providers, including unions, is to offer no-interest credit for six months or a year and then impose as much as 25 percent on the unpaid balance accumulated over that period.

13 Predictably, although the company did not summarily fire strikers, it cut down their hours or found other ways to punish them.

6. Toward a New Labor Movement, Part One

1 Following C. Wright Mills, I use the term "setup" to stand for the complex economic, political, and social power institutions that govern U.S. society.

2 For instance, in the 1930s workers and their unions were resolutely anti-war and only reversed this stance on the eve of the Japanese attack on Pearl Harbor.

3 Even today, almost fifty years after Congress passed the Civil Rights Act, most blacks are still stuck in low-paying jobs or have none. Black men are likely, during their lifetimes, to suffer imprisonment or to languish under the authority of the criminal "justice" system, or both.

4 The term "cultural capital" was coined by French sociologist Pierre Bourdieu to signify what requisites individuals and social formations needed to possess to pass examinations, advance to more elite institutions, and qualify for professional, technical, and administrative careers. Cultural capital is rarely acquired by schooling alone; most people who have knowl-edge of art, literature, current events, and history come from families that have passed down the habit of reading, conduct discussions at the dinner table, and take their children to concerts, libraries, and museums. As a rule, these households are middle class, although occasionally working-class families have acquired these practices.

5 Iowa Democratic Senator Tom Harkin introduced a bill raising the mini-mum to $10.10 an hour—still a poverty wage—and by the end of 2013 Obama seemed to ready to agree with his proposal.

6 That said, the U.S. workforce is going to have to rise up first. In the 1970s, when French and German workers' movements demanded shorter hours, their opponents invariably cited the long hours worked in U.S. industries. The French enacted a seven-hour day and retirement at sixty, but the dangerous example of the United States grows steadily worse as pressure

mounts to extend the minimum age for Social Security pay to sixty-seven or even seventy, and as part-time workers lacking guaranteed income scrabble for *more* hours. In short, the fight for shorter hours, a lower retirement age, and income guarantees is squarely in American labor's court.

7 For a powerful critique of upward mobility, one of the key elements of the American dream, see Joseph E. Stiglitz, "Equal Opportunity, Our National Myth," *New York Times*, February 17, 2013. According to Stiglitz, 42 percent of Americans born into the bottom fifth of earners never succeed in moving out of that category. "The upwardly mobile American is becoming a statistical oddity," he argues.

8 Henri Lefebvre, "The Right to the City," *Writings on Cities*, Oxford: Blackwell, 1995.

9 Over the years, housing movements have approached union pension funds for investments, with very spotty results.

10 The grocery stores of the consumer cooperative movement have spread and flourished across the United States, although the housing developments, sadly, have not.

11 Robert Pear, "New Federal Rule Requires Insurers to Offer Mental Health Coverage," *New York Times*, February 21, 2013.

12 See Stanley Aronowitz and William DiFazio, *The Jobless Future* (2nd ed.), Minneapolis: University of Minnesota Press, 2009.

13 Catherine Rampell, "It Takes a B.A. to Find a Job as a File Clerk," *New York Times*, February 20, 2013.

14 See Jonathan Bloom, "Brookwood Labor College and the Progressive Labor Network of the Interwar United States, 1921–1937," unpublished PhD dissertation, New York University, 1972.

15 The Jewish federation of the IWO was the largest, but others also thrived, especially the Finnish, Hungarian, Polish, and Ukrainian groups in Chicago, Minneapolis and Detroit.

7. Toward a New Labor Movement, Part Two

1 Two excellent works on TUEL are available. Volumes 9 and 10 of Phillip Foner's *History of the Labor Movement in the United States* (New York: International Publishers, 1991 and 1994) give an exhaustive account of TUEL and its successor, the Trade Union Unity League. James Barrett's

William Z. Foster and the Tragedy of American Communism (Urbana: University of Illinois Press, 2009) is more analytic and critical.

2 When TUEL began organizing, traditional unions condemned their affiliates as "dual" organizations.

3 Shorter hours are both necessary and desirable: necessary as the most effective solution to unemployment; desirable for the time it could afford workers to address needs and interests outside the workplace. The six-hour day is a reasonable demand for the sake of technological change and wealth accumulation that mostly lays idle.

4 At its 2013 convention, the AFL-CIO declared a modest departure from its past practices of laissez-faire and negligent organizing. The Federation showed its forward motion by electing Bhairavi Desai, executive director of New York's Taxi Workers Alliance, to its executive council and passing a series of resolutions pledging new initiatives in behalf of the largely nonunion working poor. However, commentators like Steve Early and Michael Hirsch remain skeptical about whether these brave words will be translated into action. We should welcome any steps the AFL may take, but since union power resides mainly in the affiliates, not the Federation, there is little reason to be more than somewhat hopeful.

5 A nonreformist reform is a demand that actually changes the terms and conditions of how the economic, political and social systems operate, the distribution of the economic surplus and how issues such as consumption, leisure and working life are addressed. In general, these reforms strengthen the power of labor and can diminish the power of capital.

6 At its winter 2013 meeting, the AFL-CIO executive council endorsed construction of the Keystone Pipeline, while offering hollow phrases of support for measures addressing the environmental crisis. The reason is fairly clear: in times of mass unemployment labor cannot refuse to back job creation, even if it might have serious deleterious effects on water, agriculture and other aspects of the environment.

Index